JOY AND

THE PROBLEM OF EVIL

RICK HOWE

Books by Rick Howe

Path of Life: Finding the Joy You've Always Longed For, 2012, University Ministries Press Revised Edition, 2017. 279 pages.

River of Delights: Quenching Your Thirst For Joy, Volume 1, 2015, University Ministries Press Revised Edition, 2017. 230 pages.

River of Delights: Quenching Your Thirst For Joy, Volume 2, 2015, University Ministries Press Revised Edition, 2017. 250 pages.

Living Waters: Daily Refreshment for Joyful Living, 2017, University Ministries Press. 393 pages.

Reasons of the Heart: Joy and the Rationality of Faith, 2017, University Ministries Press. 250 pages.

For Small Group Studies

Enjoying God: Discovering the Greatest of All Pleasures, University Ministries Press, 2017. 122 pages.

Love's Delights: The Joys of Marriage and Family, University Ministries Press, 2017. 104 pages.

Sacred Patterns: Work, Rest, and Play in a Joyful Vision of Life, University Ministries Press, 2017. 122 pages.

Kingdom Manifesto: A Call to Joyful Activism, University Ministries Press, 2017. 104 pages.

Joy and the Problem of Evil, University Ministries Press, Boulder, 2017. 122 pages.

For more information, visit www.rickhowe.org.

UNIVERSITY MINISTRIES PRESS
BOULDER, COLORADO
Copyright © 2017.

ISBN: 978-0-9962696-9-8

ABBREVIATIONS

NIV   New International Version

NRSV   New Revised Standard Version

RSV   Revised Standard Version

CONTENTS

AUTHOR'S NOTE

*J*oy and the Problem of Evil is the last of three sections of my work, *Reasons of the Heart: Joy and the Rationality of Faith*. Because they are foundational to this project, I have drawn from these earlier works on joy:

Rick Howe, *Path of Life: Finding the Joy You've Always Longed for* (Boulder, CO: University Ministries Press, 2017)

Rick Howe, *River of Delights: Quenching Your Thirst For Joy, Volumes 1 and 2* (Boulder, CO: University Ministries Press, 2017)

There are many endnotes in *Joy and the Problem of Evil*. They include references to scholarly works, as well as my own comments. If texts of Scripture aren't given in full in the body of the book, they have been included in the endnotes to spare you the chore of looking them up yourself. My suggestion is that you read this book first without interacting with the endnotes in order to trace the flow of thought without interruption, and then read it again with those references.

The "Questions for Thought and Discussion" at the end of each chapter reflect my hope that you will study this book with others, my belief that learning in community is the best way to learn, and my prayer that God will use this book to create communities of joy.

PREFACE

J oy fits in a world created and governed by a benevolent, wise, all-powerful God. There are good reasons to believe that such a God exists. But our world also features pain, suffering, and a troubling array of moral evil. No discussion of joy is complete without coming to grips with these stubborn facts. There can be no happily-ever-after ending to the story unless joy meets these foes on a field of battle and survives the ordeal.

There are more books and articles on the problem of evil than you could read even if you wanted to. Apart from the fact that you paid for it, why should you venture into this terrain with me? This is why: My exploration will keep joy paramount in our thinking, and you won't find that in many treatments of the subject. I am not interested in defending mere theism, or any version of Christian faith that does not see joy at the center of God's purposes for us. Nor do I have any interest in defending a vision of life that does not take seriously our cultural mandate and stewardship of the earth, which, I believe, factor significantly in the Creator's design for our joy. The final chapter of the book is not a defense, but a rallying call to followers of Christ to take action against evil as agents of God's Kingdom. It is a summons to live out Kingdom commitments to righteousness, peace, and joy in the Holy Spirit. If addressing the problem of evil does not end here, I have no desire to begin.

CHAPTER 1

A TALE WORTH TELLING,
A STORY WORTH DEFENDING

L et me begin this study by telling you the Story of joy. The narrative opens with a preface about its Author.

THEOLOGY 101: A JOYFUL GOD

God loves being God. He enjoys being God. He takes immeasurable pleasure in simply being God. Can you really imagine a God who didn't like himself? Who was frustrated or bored with having to be the Supreme Being? Can you really envision the Creator of the universe wishing that he could be someone else, somewhere else, doing something else? I can't.

The joy of God begins with his overflowing delight in himself. Augustine declared, "Thou art an everlasting joy to Thyself!"[1] Aquinas wrote: God "possesses joy in Himself and all things else for His delight." [2] It is the essence of God to be joyful.[3] He exults in his excellence. He rejoices in his regal splendor. He takes boundless pleasure in his infinite perfection. It's a good thing for us that he does! There would be no joy anywhere in the universe if he did not. Before the first word of creation, God existed eternally in a state of unimaginable, immeasurable delight.

The joy of God is Trinitarian in nature. To say that God is a Trinity is to affirm that the one God is a community of Persons – Father, Son, and Holy Spirit – who delight in each other and revel in the beatitude of their shared love.[4] There never was a time when this was not so. There never will be. If we could glimpse what angels behold, we would see that this Fellowship of Joy is a "great fountain of energy and beauty spurting up at the very centre of reality."[5] All joy flows from these Headwaters.[6]

CREATION, FALL, AND REDEMPTION

Original Joy. Once upon a time, or before there was time, there was God, and only God. Then he created. He sang a pure and powerful song, and suddenly angels surrounded his throne. Myriads of heavenly creatures. Countless ranks. As they joined his song, lending harmony to the Maker's creative melody, galaxies and stars and planets, billions upon billions, came into existence.[7] And then his musical mandate brought forth a particular world, our own, filled with plants, insects, and animals – sea-swimmers, land-walkers, and sky-flyers – as many and varied as the luminaries in the night sky. Nearly finished, he sang once more and fashioned the crown of his handiwork, humans – a man and a woman – to mirror him in his world, and to steward and rule it in his stead.

Why did God create? The answer can't be that he was lonely or bored, that it was a whim or an inadvertence, that he was somehow compelled to do it, or that there was a deficit in his existence that could only be remedied by creating a universe. None of this can be true of the Supreme Being.[8] God's life was full and complete before he spoke the first word of creation. This is the right answer to our question: God created from the plenitude of his pleasure. He created from the overflow of his joy. The universe is a surplus to him. It is "gloriously superfluous."[9] As Louis Smedes put it: God was "free to create or not to create. He did it out of his own good pleasure, for the divine fun of it."[10] This is the deep truth of the universe: God created because it was sheer delight to do so.[11]

Sometimes my heart aches for Eden. For that ancient *garden of delights*.[12] I long for the world God first created. A world unspoiled and unsullied by sin. A world filled with tokens of the divine Presence, from the shimmering light of stars overhead to the cool, crystalline dew beneath one's feet at the dawning of the day, each and every one pointing vividly and irresistibly to its Source. I yearn for the world in which the knowledge of God was untrammeled, and every blink of the eye brought one into touch with some new dimension of his glory. I long for the day long past when no distinction was even possible between sensual and spiritual, when all pleasures were joyful, directed to God in thanksgiving and praise, and joy pulsed with pleasure in the Creator and the good world that he created.[13]

Joy Lost. Alas, that world did not survive. Its brevity is linked to the mystery of human freedom. The unthinkable happened. Our forebears chose the Creator's good gifts over the Creator himself. They chose to forge their own future rather than embrace the adventures God had in store for them. They chose to write their own story rather than play a part in God's. Though it was sheer folly to do so, they turned their will away from the will of God. The harmony between Being and being was destroyed. Real pleasures were lost, and sensual idols took their place. The joy that bound creatures together and all created things to the Creator became a wistful memory. A whisper that few still hear, beckoning the heart to a better time and a better world.

Our freedom made joy possible. Our misuse of that gift shattered the fragile and precious jewel. Only shards remain, bits and pieces strewn over the sands of human experience like the remains of a long-lost and once-glorious civilization.

What great loss the Fall brought to our race!

We are used to living with our sin, like skunks at home with their own stench. We take as normal fare what the Bible treats as a great horror and scandal.[14] Nothing could be more abnormal than humanity in its fallen condition. Nothing more unnatural. In our sinful state we have exchanged the glory of God for smudgy little gods of our own making, and the wine of joy for the waste of our own perversions: an obscene draught, which, though it offends the sensibilities of heaven, we have come absurdly to prefer.

The Psalmist declares: "Those who choose another god multiply their sorrows."[15] To limit this to images of wood and stone is to miss the point. To make a god of anything other than the living and true God is to forsake the Fountain of Joy.[16] It is to drink instead from the fetid marshes of our own folly. Idols of the heart are not only tokens of defiance, but monuments to our insanity. The self-inflicted wounds of idolatry, in fact, are its greatest irony. Make a god of money and you will pierce your heart with many pangs.[17] Make a god of pleasure and you may as well try to grasp the wind in your hands.[18] Whatever our god, at whatever self-made shrine we bow, we forgo by that choice the joy for which we were created, and embrace a course that will lead only to sorrow beyond anything we can imagine. As Peter Kreeft put it, "Since an idol *is* not God, no matter how sincerely or passionately it is treated as God, it is bound to break the heart of the worshipper. . . . You can't get blood from a stone or divine joy from nondivine things."[19]

The temptation of our first parents was to become like God.[20] They were enticed to leave their station under his wise and generous rule, and to chase something they foolishly thought would be better. They thought they were pursuing a greater good; what they found was a Curse: alienation from the Creator, from themselves, from each other, and from all other creature-life.

They made themselves petty deities, and, in that choice, multiplied their sorrow. Day after day brought forth new grief, from the painful memory of Eden-lost to the horrors of their own growing evil. It is an ancient story. Every chapter tells the same tale. Only the times, places, and characters change. We are all sons of Adam and daughters of Eve. We have all shared in their sin and know their consequent sorrow.

This is the condition of fallen humanity. This is what it means to be "by nature children of wrath."[21] The wrath of God is not a bolt of lighting, thrown Zeus-like from the heavens to punish wrongdoers. *Wrath is joy rejected.*[22] Peter Kreeft is right: "But the opposite of true joy is far worse than anguish . . . . In fact, its opposite is hell."[23] Jesus' description of perdition is no pre-scientific fiction. It is as realistic as anything can be. Hell is a place of weeping and gnashing of teeth.[24] Ultimate sorrow and grief. If joy is found only in the undimmed presence of God,[25] and hell is the darkness of eternal separation from him,[26] there is no other way that it could be. Hell is the place of divine wrath: joy refused and forfeited with finality. It is the unending, unmitigated sorrow of choosing another god.[27] It became one of two destinies the day our first parents took their first steps from the Garden.[28]

Joy Regained. Fallen earth is neither Eden nor hell. Sin accounts for the first, and grace for the second. Short of hell, joy lost can be regained. In fact, this is the heart of redemption. It is God's loving action to restore sinners to the joy for which they were created.

The joy of salvation begins with the joy of the Savior. Here, as everywhere, our joy is sourced in the overflowing joy of God. His mercy is not meager, his goodness never grudging. It is lavish. Profuse. A cascading waterfall. A coursing river. A fathomless, brimming well. A life-saving, thirst-quenching drink poured into dry and desolate hearts in desperate need of refreshment.[29]

Christians believe that in Jesus God has drawn near to us, so near that he became one of us. Why? The Nicene Creed answers with the words, "For us human beings and for our salvation."[30] Our sin and misery created the need for God's action in Christ. But there is another question we should ask: Why would God do this?[31] Our need did not create an obligation for him. He could have left us in our sin and been fully just in doing so. Why did he script the drama of salvation, and in Jesus Christ step onto the stage of human history as its central character? Because it was his joy to do so!

With a sense of wonder the prophet Micah asked, "Who is a God like you, pardoning iniquity and passing over transgression?" No one! This is astonishing! Not at all what sinners should expect from a holy God! But there is an even greater wonder when we ask why God would deal with us so. Micah's answer takes us to the heart of God: "because he delights in steadfast love."[32] There is unimaginable pleasure here that only God can know. This insight into the heart of God leapt to life in the assuring words of Jesus: "Fear not, little flock, for it is the Father's good pleasure to give you the kingdom."[33] And, "Just so, I tell you there is . . . joy in heaven over one sinner who repents" (a joy pictured with music, dancing, and a feast).[34]

So great was Christ's joy in bringing salvation to the world that even the agony of the cross was compelled to yield to it. The author of Hebrews wrote of him: "For the joy that was set before him [he] endured the cross, despising the shame, and is seated at the right hand of the throne of God."[35] It was the vision of his redemptive work completed that brought him such joy, even in the hour of his greatest suffering and pain. If we cannot fathom his passion (and we cannot), we will never plumb his greater pleasure in its outcome. Nevertheless, the joy of salvation begins here. Our boon in redemption lies in the bountiful joy of the Redeemer.

God enjoys bringing salvation to sinners, and sinners to salvation. It is a joy for him to renovate human hearts, opening them to all he has done, all that he is now doing, and all that he has pledged to do. Our joy starts here. When grace triumphs in us, we come to revel in our need for God. Our plight brings us pleasure.[36] We experience grace as a feast offered to poor, famished, thirsty wayfarers a step away from perishing in their desperate want:

> Ho everyone who thirsts,
>   come to the waters;
> and you that have no money,
>   come, buy and eat!
> Come, buy wine and milk
>   without money and without price.
> Why do you spend your money for that which is not bread,
>   and your labor for that which does not satisfy?
> Listen carefully to me, and eat what is good,
>   and delight yourselves in rich food.
> Incline your ear, and come to me;
>   listen so that you may live. (Isaiah 55:1-3, NRSV)

In our sin we are utterly lost and ruined, without hope because we fully deserve the trouble we are in and can do nothing to change it. Nothing to escape it. We cannot see a light, and could not move toward it even if we did. Sin brings only unrelenting darkness and despair. And then. And then God. And then God transforms our troubled lot. He pardons us! Rescues us! Delivers us! He reaches down to us when we could not reach up to him. He meets us in our misery. He sings to us, sings over us, and puts his song within us. We are enchanted by the music. He washes away the filth that caked us. Mends our brokenness. Dresses and heals our wounds. Clothes our nakedness in robes that befit royalty. Fills our aching and empty souls. Quenches our terrible thirst. Then, to our utter amazement, he invites us into an "ecstasy of love and delight," C.S. Lewis wrote, "compared with which the most rapturous love between a man and a woman on this earth is

9

mere milk and water."[37] Hands that covered our face in shame now lift in grateful praise, and we join Mary's song: "My soul magnifies the Lord, and my spirit rejoices in God my Savior!"[38]

The joy of salvation is a restoration of joy in the Triune God. It is not the kind of joy we experience in viewing a sunset or a meadow of alpine flowers. It is more like the gaiety of a wedding dance: delighting in one's beloved and the celebration of love and life together. The joy of salvation is a participation in God's joy: the Father's joy in the Son and the Spirit, the Son's joy in the Father and the Spirit, the Spirit's joy in the Father and the Son, and the shared joy of the Three-in-One. Sin destroyed the communion of joy our kind once shared with this Three-Personal God.[39] Redemption restores it. We are brought back to, and drawn into, this Fellowship, or Dance, of joy. Joy is then experienced in its highest and purest form as love's delight: joy in God's Triune love for us, our small, growing love offered back to the Father, Son, and Holy Spirit, and the love and joy we share with all who have entered into the life of God.[40]

JOY AND OUR CULTURAL MANDATE

Joy's Story is not complete unless we include God's vision for the world and the role he has called us to play. The Creator has plans for us. Some have your name on them. Some have mine. But he also has purposes for image-bearers-as-a-whole, also known as the human race. His design embraces all people, and the earth as our shared habitat. This finds expression in a mandate that was given at the beginning of our story.

> Then God said, "Let us make man in our image, after our likeness. And let them have dominion over the fish of the sea and over the birds of the heavens and over the livestock and over all the earth and over every creeping thing that creeps on the earth." (Genesis 1:26)

> So God created man in his own image,
>   in the image of God he created him;

male and female he created them. (Genesis 1:27)

And God blessed them. And God said to them, "Be fruitful and multiply and fill the earth and subdue it, and have dominion over the fish of the sea and over the birds of the heavens and over every living thing that moves on the earth." (Genesis 1:28)

The world is not ours; it is God's.[41] We are managers, not owners. An important part of what it means to be made in God's image lies in the charge to rule the earth in God's stead, fulfilling his vision for our planet and the human project. We obey this mandate from the Creator when we discover resources and develop the potential he put into his world, when we harness all things for his glory and the good of all, and we do it in a way that honors, protects, and preserves the world he made and has entrusted to us.

Goodness, beauty, and truth. The ancient Greeks saw goodness, beauty, and truth as pure, transcendent realities that shape our experience in the world.[42] Whatever we find to be good in our world is an instance of the Good, which is timeless and supreme. The beautiful in our experience participates in Beauty, above and beyond our sentience. Whatever is true is grounded in absolute, eternal, and unchanging Truth. Augustine and other theologians embraced this, but taught that the one God, the Creator of the world, is the transcendent Source of all goodness, beauty, and truth in it.[43]

The people of faith whose stories and songs are written in the Bible didn't think about these things abstractly (or if they did, they didn't leave us a record of their thoughts). But if you had asked them if God is good, they would have said, "Taste and see!"[44] If you asked if God is beautiful, they would have said, "Breathtakingly!" And if you had asked them if God is truthful, they would have exclaimed, "Absolutely!" If you asked them how they knew these things, they wouldn't have constructed a chain of reasoning to get them to those conclusions, they would have talked about God's gracious self-disclosure and their matching experience in worship and life.

Goodness, beauty, and truth are united in our Creator. They are treasures from him and portals to him. They are structural to the world that he intends for us. They are essential to the mandate he has given us and are central to our joy. They are meant to shape and inform all that we do as his image-bearers. In every endeavor we should ask, "Does this reflect the goodness of God, and his commitment to the well-being of all people? Does it reflect God's commitment to beauty in the world? Does it align with what God has revealed to be true about himself, our world, and the nature and purpose of human life?"

If our cultural mandate were put into a global mission statement, it would look something like this:

- Vision: to become a fully developed world in harmony with God and his purposes.

- Mission: to steward the resources of the world for the glory of God and the good of all.

- Core Values: goodness, beauty, and truth.

- Intended Outcome: Global joy.

Can you imagine a world in which all endeavors seek to bring this vision about? A world in which all projects are harnessed to this mission? A world in which all enterprises are shaped by these foundational values? A world that flourishes in joy as a result? This is what God has purposed for us from the beginning.

STEWARDS OF THE EARTH

If we look at the world through the lens of joy we will see God in all that we behold. In its vastness we will see his immensity. In its great antiquity we will see his eternal power. In its grandeur we will see his glory. In its wonders we will see his wisdom. In its intricacies we will see his genius. In its wildness we will see his sovereign freedom and surprising ways. In its pleasures we will see his goodness to us. If we see the world as it truly is, we will see it enchanted with the presence of God.[45]

If our first response to the world is anything but reverence, wonder, and awe, we haven't seen it truly. We are out of touch with reality. There is much that we will miss and much that we will misuse because we misunderstand the true nature and significance of the world. We will live in it like witless thugs throwing fine crystal into the air for target practice.

God invites us to savor his world and calls us to steward it. Our first calling as bearers of God's image is to govern the world as a theater for his glory.[46] We should do nothing to diminish it. Nothing to disgrace it. Nothing to sully it. Nothing to spoil it. We should do everything we can to protect it. Everything we can to preserve it. We should use but not abuse. We should enjoy but not exploit. Because it bears the presence of God, the earth is sacred. Because it is a habitation of God, it is holy. Our stewardship begins here.

Our responsibility to steward the earth includes managing its resources for the good of all. God does not intend that some (who happen to have and control wealth) should enjoy the benefits of his world and others (who do not) should not. Nor does he intend that one generation should tap the resources of his world in a way that deprives future generations of them.[47] It isn't our planet. We don't have that right:

> The earth is the LORD's and the fullness thereof,
>   the world and those who dwell therein. (Psalm 24:1)

> One generation shall laud your works to another,
>   and shall declare your mighty acts. (Psalm 145:4)

It should come as no surprise that our stewardship of the earth is meant to reflect the two great commandments we have been given: to love God fully and supremely, and to love our neighbors as ourselves.[48] We are called to manage the resources of the world as an expression of love for our Maker. We are summoned to steward its provisions as an expression of love for our neighbor – near and far, present and future. This is integral to our joy and God's glory in the world.

JOY AND THE GOOD LIFE

Why should we embrace this Story? First, because it is true, and then because we will flourish in life if we do. First, because it truly illumines the landscape of our hearts and our experience in the world, and then because we will discover life at its best if we do.

Joy and the *telos* of life. When ancient Greek philosophers thought of the ultimate object or aim of something, they used the word *telos*, which literally means "an end." When they spoke of our *telos* as human beings, they were talking about the point of human life, or the meaning or purpose of our existence. To pursue our final end, to fulfill our great purpose (which, for instance, Aristotle saw as living according to reason and virtue) is to live well and to flourish in life (which, according to Aristotle, is another way of describing happiness).

The people of the ancient Jewish Scriptures envisioned life differently. To them, life is like a journey. Living is like walking.[49] If we take a journey we must choose a path. The path we choose depends on the destination we hope to reach. The path one takes in the journey of life (as opposed to a trip to a neighboring village) is the "path of life." In many ways it comes to the same thing as the Greek's *telos*: It is about direction and a destination. Its concern is the meaning, purpose, and goal of life. Unlike the Greeks, however, Jewish people believed that the path of life is revealed. Reason doesn't discover it; we don't stumble upon it; God makes it known.

The path of life is not about human potential and achievement. It isn't about happiness as the Greek philosophers understood it. It is about a relationship with God and the life-encompassing joy we discover there:

> You show to me the path of life.
> In your presence there is fullness of joy;
>   in your right hand are pleasures forevermore. (Psalm 16:11, NRSV)

In this vision of life, joy is our final end, our *telos*, the meaning of our existence.[50] People who live well enjoy God and the good gifts he bestows.

Joy and the *summum bonum* of life. Another way of talking about the good life frames the issue in terms of our *summum bonum*, or our greatest good. There are many goods in the world: food, clothing, friends, knowledge, and health. A good is anything that has positive value for human life. What is it that distinguishes our greatest good from other goods? Aristotle taught that a final good is one that is desired for its own sake, and not for the sake of anything else. Other things may be related to it as means, but it will never be a means to anything else because there is nothing higher or better.[51] The only thing that meets this requirement, according to Aristotle, is happiness. All other goods are means to this end.

Christians say that God is the Greatest Good. There are two sides to this coin, however. Objectively, God is the greatest good in this world, and must be in any world that he creates. But if we are talking about the greatest good *for us*, it must engage us as subjects. It must involve us in an enjoyment of this good.[52] God is *the* Greatest Good; enjoying him is *our* greatest good. Seeking this is the good life; finding it is life at its very best.

The glory of God and our joy. The Westminster Shorter Catechism approaches the good life by asking the question, "What is the chief end of man?" and then answering, "Man's chief end is to glorify God, and to enjoy him forever." We glorify God as *the* Greatest Good when we enjoy him as *our* greatest good.[53]

What is the link between God's glory and our joy, and how does it help us understand and pursue the good life? Although the word *glory* can be used of the revelation of God's presence in the world, in its primary theological sense glory characterizes God-as-he-is-in-himself.[54] It is his majesty, his magnificence, his infinite worth, and unlimited power. It is all that God is in his transcendence over his creation. Like the holiness of God, the glory of God is not a single attribute, but his very essence. It is his nature in its totality. In all that he is he is glorious. The Biblical writers tried to capture something of this when they called him "the King of glory,"[55] "the God of glory,"[56] the "Father of glory,"[57] and "the Majestic Glory."[58]

The fitting response to the glory of God is reverence, wonder, and awe: a shudder at our own smallness, a shivering sense of the magnitude of God, and a trembling delight in his unbounded greatness and grandeur. Hearts that have been gripped by glory know the tremulous joy that so great a Being exists, and astonishment-that-takes-one's-breath-away that so great a God would invite us to know and enjoy him. It is a pleasure that is at once dread and delight, fear and fascination, amazement and adoration. To glorify God is to acknowledge, confess, celebrate, and live our lives in light of God's glory. This is joy's native habitat, its indigenous environment.

The supremacy of love. No vision of the good life can claim to be Christian unless it centers on what Jesus saw as God's chief concern for our lives. He summed it up this way:

> You shall love the Lord your God with all your heart and with all
> your soul and with all your mind. This is the great and first
> commandment. And a second is l ike it: You shall love your

neighbor as yourself. On these two commandments depend all the
Law and the Prophets. (Matthew 22:37-40)

This is not something different from what we have already learned about the
good life. It is another way of talking about the same thing. In fact, the best
way to understand these love commands is to retrace our steps. Loving God
is a path of life, a way of living in the world. It is finding the meaning and
purpose of our existence in relation to God and in a relationship with him,
gratefully embracing the joy of his presence and the pleasures he bestows. It
is regarding God as the Greatest Good, and reveling in him as our greatest
good. It is cherishing him in his infinite worth, putting him first in our
thoughts, first in our loves and affections, first in our values and priorities,
first in our interests and concerns, and first in all that we hope for and aspire
to in life. Loving God is exulting in his glory, exalting him in his majesty,
and making our way of life a fitting response so that others see and are
inspired to join us in giving him praise.[59]

It might be tempting to stop there, but Jesus did not. For him, loving
God includes loving the people he places in our lives. We love them by
affirming their value and developing relational virtues, such as kindness,
generosity, humility, and forbearance that enable us to live together robustly
in God's world. It is more than this, however. We love others when we
include them in our fulfillment of the cultural mandate and our calling to
steward the earth. Both are world-affirming and life-shaping. Both are
meant to be expressions of love. Both are essential to our joy and theirs.

This is the Tale worth telling. This is the Story I will gladly defend.

QUESTIONS FOR THOUGHT AND DISCUSSION

1. What do you think about the relationship between our joy and a joyful God?

2. What do you think about the author's treatment of joy as the central theme of Creation, the Fall, and Redemption?

3. What implications does the "cultural mandate" have for your understanding of the "human project?"

4. How do you see our stewardship of the earth and its implications for joy?

5. What is the significance of joy for your understanding of the good life?

CHAPTER 2

LAY OF THE LAND
AND FIRST DEFENSE:
DIVINE OMNIPOTENCE

N ow you know something of joy's Story. In this chapter and the next I will respond to its critics: not their criticism of details in the narrative, but its major premise and central theme: the existence of a good, all-powerful God who created and governs the world. This critique is known as the problem of evil, a collection of arguments against the existence of such a God from the presence of evil in the world. Its centerpiece is a claim that there is a contradiction in this package of propositions:

(1) God exists.
(2) God is all-powerful.
(3) God is good.
(4) Evil exists.

If there is a contradiction here, it doesn't lie on the surface. None of these claims contradicts another. True, critics say, but the second and third assertions have implications that make the contradiction clear. We can restate the problem this way:

(1) God exists.
(2) God is all-powerful.
    (2.1) An all-powerful God could eliminate evil.
(3) God is good.
    (3.1) A good God would eliminate evil.
(4) Evil exists.

This is the logical problem of evil: If evil exists (4), and it is true that an all-powerful God could eliminate evil (2.1), and that a good God would eliminate evil (3.1), then it cannot also be true that God exists (1), or if he does, that he is all-powerful (2) or good (3). Though many claim that this argument vanquishes Christian faith, we will see that for every thrust of its sharp blade there is a successful parry. As a deductive proof, the problem of evil is daunting but not ultimately dangerous to belief in a good, all-powerful God.

Even if that proof fails, however, the problem of evil cannot be dismissed so easily. An argument can fail as a strict logical proof and still be a strong argument.[1] (There is a strong case for the existence of God, even if its outcome is not logically certain.[2]) This leads us to a second version of the case against God known as the evidential problem of evil. One argument looks like this, with a theological premise, followed by a factual claim and a conclusion.

(1) If a good, all-powerful God exists, then no gratuitous evil exists;
(2) Gratuitous evil exists;
(3) Therefore, a good, all-powerful God does not exist.

When we look at our world, critics say, the magnitude of evil and the horrendous and apparent gratuitous character of much of it makes the existence of a good, all-powerful God less probable than his non-existence. I will endeavor to persuade you that though it seems compelling to many, this argument fails, as well.

Finally, there is the emotional or existential problem of evil. Some people are haunted by the questions, "Why do the wicked prosper?"[3] And "Why do the righteous suffer?"[4] They cannot bring themselves to believe in a good, all-powerful God because they have been victimized by injustice or traumatized by suffering and pain. They have endured hardship, someone they love has suffered, or they have just seen too much evil in the world. The question "Why?" overwhelms their ability or inclination to believe. If that describes you, I can sit with you in your pain, but I can't give you reasons, specific to you, that God has for allowing these things in your experience. I am only a fellow traveler on the path of life. If you walk with me, however, I can tell you how many have experienced joy in the midst of suffering and pain, and invite you to join our company. If there is good news in your bad news, it is that joy is meant for just such times.[5]

EVIL

Since we are exploring evil and the existence of God, we should begin by getting clear about the notion of evil. The word can be used with moral and non-moral meanings. In a Christian vision of life, *moral* evil refers to a character trait or the property of an action (or inaction) for which a moral agent is responsible, that is incompatible with God's character and will, and that directly or indirectly brings harm into his world. Human violence is an example of moral evil. *Natural* evil, in contrast, refers to pain and suffering that happens not as a result of human agency, but of natural forces under the governance of the Creator. Earthquakes, hurricanes, tornadoes, floods, and disease are examples of this kind of evil (though we will qualify this below).

The peculiar nature of moral evil. Some people think of good and evil as if they were equal but opposite traits, as if they were diametrically opposed in moral status, but the same in ontological status (that is, as if they had equal standing with respect to their existence in the world). Picture two mounted knights side by side, identical in every way except the color of their steeds and standards, one light and the other dark, and the causes to which they are committed, one benevolent, the other bent on harm.[6]

Does evil exist in the same way that good does? It does not.

Goodness is eternal because it is an attribute of the everlasting God; evil, on the other hand, is temporal. It began at a point in the history of the cosmos. This is where the path takes a surprising turn. Evil had a beginning, but not as a creation of God. How can this be? How can something begin to exist in God's universe and not be his creation? We must start here: If everything created by God is good, as Christians affirm, then whatever evil is, it cannot be a creation of God.[7]

It is a popular mistake to think of evil as a being, or an entity. It is not. Moral evil is a character trait and the property of an action for which moral agents are responsible. When we speak of evil people or evil beings, they are evil in the sense that they have developed a twisted disposition that results in twisted actions. God takes responsibility for creating moral agents who, in their freedom, can do evil and become evil, and for sovereignly permitting their warped character and misdeeds, but evil is their own making, not God's.[8]

Evil exists, but not properly or natively as a being, an entity, or a thing in itself. It is a corruption of something good. A perversion. C.S. Lewis wrote, "Evil is a parasite, not an original thing. The powers which enable evil to carry on are powers given it by goodness. All the things which enable a bad man to be effectively bad are in themselves good things – resolution, cleverness, good looks, existence itself."[9] Evil is an interloper. A thief. It has nothing of its own. It must borrow or steal from God's good world to accomplish its ends.

Demonic evil. From a Christian perspective, humans aren't the only finite moral agents who are responsible for evil in God's world. At least some, and perhaps much, of what we perceive to be natural evil because it is unrelated to human agency is moral evil on a higher plane. In another book, I wrote:

> If we could part the curtains that hide the unseen spiritual realm and see what is behind the woes of our world, we would see a rejection of God and his ways. And behind that we would see his ancient adversary blinding eyes, hardening hearts, and stirring a pot of malice that spills into our world. He is known by many names in the Scriptures: Lucifer, Satan, the devil, the evil one, the tempter, the accuser, the dragon, the father of lies, the god of this world. With legions of angelic beings who followed him in a primordial rebellion against God, he is bent on deflecting worship from God, defying the will of God, and destroying God's world.
>
> His kingdom is dark; his reign, sinister. His power is great; his rage, greater. In a hymn for the ages, Luther wrote of him: "For still our ancient foe doth seek to work us woe; his craft and power are great, and armed with cruel hate, on earth is not his equal."[10]

In the biblical narrative, Satan and demons are causal agents in the world, bringing about catastrophe, human sickness, and even animal pain and death.[11] In our limitations we are not in a position to quantify evil in the world that can be traced to malevolent spiritual beings; nevertheless, this must be factored into a Christian understanding of evil in the world.[12]

Evil and the Fall. In a Christian vision of life, we are not what we were created to be, and so the world in which we live is not what God created it to be. Theologians describe the primordial turn of events that led to this as "the Fall."[13] Like our first parents, we have fallen from the high purposes of our Creator and have been seriously injured from the fall. The Bible uses the word "death" to describe this condition: alienation from God, from each other, from our environment, and a disintegration and dysfunction within ourselves that impacts both our bodies and our souls.[14] Much of what we consider natural evil is fall-out from the solidarity of the human race in a sinful condition: sickness, disease, infirmity, and, ultimately, the demise of our bodies.[15]

You might reject and even ridicule such notions, but that is irrelevant in this context, since it is the Christian who is being charged with contradictory beliefs. I did not create the doctrine of the Fall to maneuver around charges in the problem of evil. It is part of a rich tradition that Christians have embraced for centuries. We believe that it helps explain the world better than any other point of view. It is a more powerful, illuminating story than any other. You may not share this belief with us, but when it is brought to the problem of evil, it is a significant factor in defeating the claim that our beliefs are mutually exclusive.

Evil and our cultural mandate. We can imagine a world inhabited by creatures that seek only their own good or the good of their own brood or herd. That is not God's plan for our world, with creatures made in his image its crest. The Creator has commissioned us to be his representative, governing his world in his stead. He has entrusted us with a world-shaping project. He has called us to make something of his world from the resources of his world for the good of all people in his world. Guided by goodness, beauty, and truth, we are called to build civilizations, create cultures and institutions, and engage in enterprises that honor our Creator and bring about a world in which all people flourish in joy.

Great good can come from this. Great evil exists in the world because we have failed to deliver on this mandate. This is where we should locate structural evil, violence, and injustice. It is evil that arises from, and is perpetuated by, social institutions. The social configuration may be a family, a clan, a corporation, or a government. It may involve domestic abuse, racism, sexism, terrorism, oppression of the poor, slavery, drug and human trafficking, and even genocide. Because sin permeates all human beings,[16] it pervades all human institutions and impacts all who participate in them. Joy that could be ours has been lost.

Evil and our stewardship of the earth. The earth is host to an intricate network of ecosystems in which we play a pivotal role. In this finely tuned arrangement, we are psychosomatic beings who relate to our world in psychosomatic ways. Physical and spiritual dimensions are thread and strand in the fabric of human nature and our interaction with the world. They can and do affect each other. In our own case, if we mishandle stress (a spiritual issue), it can impact our physical health. If we cultivate bitterness, resentment, suspicion, mistrust, or anxiety (spiritual issues), it will diminish our physical well-being. It is also true that prayer and meditation have physical benefits. Joy contributes to the health of our bodies.[17] The Creator designed us this way.

If this is so, it should not be surprising that our interface with the world is both physical and spiritual. Our joy and the wellness of the world are connected.[18] There is a nexus between our sin and the world's malaise.[19] It is not only what we do in our greed (exploiting others and natural resources), but greed itself, that tears the fabric of the world. It is not only what we do in our quest for pleasure (which results in a culture of consumption, massive landfills, and ground and water pollution) that injures the earth, that false spiritual quest itself rends the intricate web of life on our planet. It is not only what we do in our arrogance that harms the world, arrogance itself causes the world to limp.[20]

We are the ones who have introduced toxins in our environment. We have ravaged and exploited the resources of the earth, and destroyed delicate ecosystems that are essential to our environment and our well-being. In ways that we must rue, we have failed in our stewardship of the earth. Evil is the result.[21]

Evil and the good life. Our understanding of the good life is critically important here. If we see pleasure as our highest good, then pain is a big problem! If God is committed to a hedonistic vision of life for us, either his plan is a poor fit for our world (He is not wise.), or he does a poor job implementing it (He is not omnipotent.). If we think that happiness is our highest good and see it in the superficial way that many do, we end up with a theological vision described by C.S. Lewis:

> What would really satisfy us would be a God who said of anything we happened to like doing, "What does it matter so long as they are contented?" We want, in fact, not so much a Father in Heaven as a grandfather in heaven - a senile benevolence who, as they say, liked to see young people enjoying themselves" and whose plan for the universe was simply that it might be truly said at the end of each day, "a good time was had by all".[22]

Joy is the *telos* of human existence, or our chief end. It is the centerpiece and crown of the good life. Life as God designed it is a quest to discover this highest and best of all pleasures.[23] God is *the* Greatest Good. He becomes *our* greatest good when we enjoy him and value him above everything else (including an untroubled life). Our greatest joy comes as we seek the glory of God in all that we do and in all that comes our way (including troubles).

This puts evil into a different framework. It invites other questions and suggests different answers than we would find with other versions of the good life. We should see evil as anything that frustrates the realization of our greatest good. It is anything that keeps us, or others, from joy.[24] If this is so, then some things that we may not have regarded as evil *per se* (good things misplaced in our values) are, because they block our path to joy. Some things that we have regarded as evil (pain and suffering), are not inherently so because they may lead us into greater experiences of joy.

MORAL FREEDOM

When I say that God created us with free will, I mean, first, that we can choose one thing and not another without anything but our own agency determining our decision, and second, that in any decision we have made, given the same conditions, we could have chosen otherwise.[25] In biblical narratives, God holds people accountable for their decisions and judges them for their misdeeds. The implication is that they were responsible for their decisions, and that they could and should have chosen differently.

I can imagine a world in which all creatures were programmed, as we might devise robots to do tasks we assign to them. Some of these creatures might be designed to build cities and bridges and roads. Some might even play musical instruments, draw, paint, sculpt, develop civilizations, and simulate cultures. But robots are not moral agents. In a world of automata, God alone would be responsible. You might wish for a world without freedom (though I find that hard to believe), but that isn't our world. God had something higher and nobler for us in mind.

This kind of freedom is essential to relationships of love, whether it is our relationship with God or with each other. Coerced love is a contradiction in terms. Love must be freely given, and if this is so, it can also be withheld. Love must be freely received, and if this is so, it can also be rejected. You might wish for a loveless world (again, I find that hard to believe), but that isn't our world. God had something far better for us in mind.[26]

27

AN ALL-POWERFUL GOD

Christians assert that the one God is infinite in power. An omnipotent God brought the universe with its billions of galaxies into being. An omnipotent God sustains this vast expanse – billions of light years from one side to another – in every moment and in every place. An omnipotent God is guiding the course of history to an end that he has determined will come to pass.

An omnipotent God could eliminate evil, critics say. Because evil exists, an omnipotent God does not. In response, we should start by getting clear about the meaning of omnipotence. The Bible affirms that God is omnipotent and that there are things an omnipotent God cannot do. He cannot lie; [27] he cannot change; [28] he cannot deny himself. [29] These observations have led theologians from Aquinas on to refine the meaning of omnipotence from the ability to do anything, to the ability to do anything that is possible.[30] God cannot not exist.[31] He cannot become dependent upon something else for his existence.[32] He cannot become more or less than he is.[33] He cannot cease being Triune.[34] These are absolute impossibilities and imply nothing about a measurement of power.[35] Nor can God do what is logically impossible. He cannot create a universe that has no beginning. He cannot draw a four-sided triangle, or a square circle, or make the statement 2+2=5 true. These are not tests of power, but tomfoolery with words.

FIRST DEFENSE: DIVINE OMNIPOTENCE

Moral evil. Critics contend that an all-powerful God could eliminate evil in the world. But if an omnipotent God cannot do what is logically impossible, then he cannot eliminate evil that results directly or indirectly from moral agency that is free in the way that I have described it. God cannot create moral agents who are free to choose good or evil and at the same time infallibly guarantee (or otherwise bring it about) that they will always choose good and never evil. C.S. Lewis put it this way:

> [God's] Omnipotence means power to do all that is intrinsically possible, not to do the intrinsically impossible. You may attribute miracles to Him, but not nonsense. There is no limit to His power.

> If you choose to say, 'God can give a creature free will and at the same time withhold free will from it,' you have not succeeded in saying anything about God: meaningless combinations of words do not suddenly acquire meaning simply because we prefix to them the two other words, 'God can.'

> It remains true that all things are possible with God: the intrinsic impossibilities are not things but nonentities. It is no more possible for God than for the weakest of His creatures to carry out both of two mutually exclusive alternatives; not because His power meets an obstacle, but because nonsense remains nonsense even when we talk it about God.[36]

This accounts for moral evil, and for some (possibly much) of what we call natural evil if it can be traced to human factors, such as the impact of human activity on our natural environment. It includes a wide array of harm, from unkind words to terrorism, from petty theft to weapons of mass destruction, from frivolous lawsuits to genocide. It includes pain and suffering brought about by toxins in our food, hazardous chemicals in our soil and water, pollution in our air, the widespread destruction of jungles and forests, and the warming of the earth's climates.[37] Illnesses that result from lifestyle choices and psychosomatic maladies belong in this category, as well. Wittingly or not, we do these things to ourselves. Christians lament all of these evils, rejoice that God is omnipotent and good, and maintain that there is no contradiction in doing both.

The debate doesn't end there, however. Another version of the argument takes us into the rarefied air of logically possible worlds. It begins with a modest claim: It is logically possible for a free-willed moral agent to choose good once. Now, if it is logically possible for a morally free agent to choose good once, then it is logically possible for that same agent to choose good every time. We aren't talking about the likelihood of this happening, and not at all about a guarantee beforehand that it will. It is a logical possibility. Critics say that we should take this a step further. If it is logically possible for one moral agent with free will to do this, then it is logically possible for a world to be populated solely with moral agents with free will and a perfect record of choosing good. An omnipotent God, critics say, could create such a logically possible world, and a good God would.[38] That we have our world instead is proof that an omnipotent, good God does not exist.

This argument has two serious flaws. First, if it is logically possible that there is a world inhabited only by morally free creatures who always choose good, it is also logically possible that there is no such world.[39] (If *S* is the set of logically possible moral agents with free will who always choose good and never evil, *S* may have members and may have none. There is no contradiction in affirming either.) It is logically possible that all moral agents who have the property of being free also have the property of choosing evil, and that this is so in every logically possible world in which they exist. If this is so, then it is possible that God cannot create a world inhabited exclusively by morally free agents with a perfect record of always choosing good and never evil.[40] The contest of logical possibilities ends in a draw (which is a win for Christian faith because this attempt to defeat it has failed).[41]

Second, critics have set the bar too low in their insistence that God should have created a better world than ours. God is not merely strong; he is omnipotent. He is not merely good; he is supremely good. An omnipotent, supremely good God must create the best of all possible worlds if it is logically possible to do so. That possibility does not exist, however, even for a God with unlimited power:

> (1) An all-powerful God can create the best of all possible worlds if it is logically possible to do so;
> (2) It is not logically possible to create the best of all possible worlds;
> (3) Therefore, an all-powerful God cannot create the best of all possible worlds.[42]

It is not logically possible to create the best of all possible worlds, because there is a contradiction embedded in the notion. A possible world can always be improved by the addition of one more logically possible, morally free agent who always chooses good, *ad infinitum*, and this will be true of any candidate for the best of all possible worlds. Thus, if X is the best of all possible worlds, then X is not (and cannot be) the best of all possible worlds.[43] Therein lies the contradiction.

In sum, it is possible that God cannot create a world populated solely by free moral agents with a perfect record of choosing good and never evil, because it is logically possible that no such world exists. Nor is it a slight to God to say that he cannot create the best of all possible worlds. Even an omnipotent God cannot do what is logically impossible. This should put an end to such nonsense, as Lewis would have put it.

Finally, let's return to the critic's notion of a logically possible world in which all inhabitants are free-willed moral agents who always choose good and never evil. The one thing we know is that ours is not that world. If such a world was possible and you could ask God to substitute it for ours, would you? Before you do, keep in mind that you, with your lifetime of decisions – some good, some bad – would not be included. Neither would anyone else you know. None of your friends. None of your family. No one in the world as we know it. If I could ask God to replace our world with that possible world, I wouldn't do it. I might be wrong, but I don't think that you would either. That is an implicit endorsement of the world God created, whatever critics may say.

Natural evil. Since we have defined natural evil as pain and suffering that happens as a result of natural forces, and is not directly or indirectly related to the volition of anyone but God, who is sovereign over the natural world, it follows that an omnipotent God can eliminate such evil. That he does not always do so shifts the argument to the goodness of God, which we will explore in the next two chapters.

QUESTIONS FOR THOUGHT AND DISCUSSION

1. Summarize the three kinds of argument against God from the existence of evil. Which connects with you the most? In what ways?

2. Discuss the differences between moral and natural evil. Which seems like more of a problem to you?

3. Do you believe in demonic evil? If so, what difference does it make for your understanding of the problem of evil? If not, are you open to that possibility?

4. How do you understand the omnipotence of God? After reading this chapter, what do you think its implications are for the problem of evil?

5. How do you understand the nature of moral freedom? What difference does it make for the problem of evil?

CHAPTER 3

SECOND DEFENSE: DIVINE GOODNESS

Christians believe that God is good. We affirm that He is infinitely worthy, supremely valuable, surpassingly desirable, and unrivaled in moral beauty. In this belief we also affirm that God is the Source of everything good in the universe, and that he is benevolent toward us and generous in his gifts. We teach our children to pray, "God is great, God is good, and we thank him for our food."[1] This belief lies at the heart of our worship:

> Oh, taste and see that the LORD is good! (Psalm 34:8)

> Praise the LORD!
> Oh give thanks to the LORD, for he is good,
>   for his steadfast love endures forever! (Psalm 106:1)

If you affirm the goodness of God, should you accept the critic's claim that a good God would eliminate evil? Or, if you accept the conclusion I reached about omnipotence in the last chapter, should you concede that a good God would eliminate all the evil he possibly can? I wouldn't if I were you.

Let's start with what we know from family life. Good parents sometimes allow their children to go through painful situations. It requires careful discernment, but if they choose not to prevent such experiences, it is because they believe that these ordeals may bring about a greater good, such as the development of character, endurance, or wisdom in facing the challenges of life. Or consider this: I still have memories of carrying a frightened, tearful child into a doctor's office for an immunization shot. I permitted a small pain in order to prevent greater pain and suffering from childhood diseases. In the language of philosophers, justifications like these constitute "morally sufficient reasons" for permitting evil. They create possibilities of greater good or prevent possibilities of greater evil.

The question before us is whether God has morally sufficient reasons for permitting evil in the world. Believers say that he does. We contend that a good, omniscient, and all-powerful God knows that a world laden with possibilities of good and evil brought about by creatures with free will is better than a world without moral freedom. In itself it is a greater good, and it creates possibilities of greater good. Though evil followed, and God knew that it would, this is the morally sufficient reason behind the creation narrative, "Then God said, "Let us make humankind in our image, according to our likeness.""[2] Not surprisingly, this claim is contested.

Philosophers say that evil is gratuitous if there is no morally sufficient reason for permitting it. It is gratuitous if it does not serve a greater good that would not otherwise come about, or prevent a greater evil that would otherwise take place.[3] The critic's argument is not that there are no instances of evil in which a greater good might result, or a greater evil might be averted, but that there are many (too many, critics say) instances of evil in which this is not the case. What possible good, they ask, can come from the torture of an infant, or the raping and killing a young girl? What greater evil is prevented?[4] A good God would not allow these things in his world.

Any response to such pain and suffering risks making light of the problem. We should weep with those who weep.[5] When we have finished weeping, however, there is an intellectual challenge to be met. There is a charge that must be answered.

THE PROBLEM OF GRATUITOUS EVIL

Now that the notion of gratuitous evil has been introduced, we can state the problem this way:

(1) If a good, all-powerful God exists, then no gratuitous evil exists;
(2) Gratuitous evil exists;
(3) Therefore, a good, all-powerful God does not exist.

I grant that this proof is formally valid, and acknowledge that many find it persuasive. I suggest, however, if the truth were fully known, that the argument is compelling to many for reasons that have nothing to do with logic.

In my book, *Reasons of the Heart: Joy and the Rationality of Faith*, I explore the relationship between emotions and beliefs, and the way they influence each other in our understanding of the world.[6] There is no way to avoid this, nor should we want to. It is true to who we are as affective-rational beings. This is nowhere clearer than when we talk about suffering and pain, whether it is our own or the experience of another. Our emotions are engaged, often in powerful ways. Whether it is "Man's inhumanity to man," as Robert Burns put it, congenital leukemia, a slow, painful death from pancreatic cancer, or the aftermath of a tsunami or an earthquake, the first response of most people to suffering is a strong desire to see it end. If it doesn't, their next response is likely to be sorrow, followed by anger. The questions may be mute, but they stir deep within: "What did she do to deserve this?" "What good can possibly come from that?"[7]

Even if we bring reason into the discussion, the conversation began with our emotions. Whatever reason may suggest for understanding suffering and pain, it will have to deal with emotions already in play. I understand that. I embrace it. I believe that it is largely what makes this argument seem compelling.[8] I offer this not as a critique, but as an observation in the interests of intellectual honesty.

Another reason this argument seems compelling is that it has a common-sense plausibility. It fits what many people perceive about the world and expect to be the case. We see evil. We may not be able to see a greater good that has come from it, or a greater evil that has been prevented.[9] The evil we see trumps the possibilities we cannot see. The first is often regarded as the *real world*, the second as nothing more than wishful thinking. In hundreds of ways this belief is reinforced in the way many are taught to manage the circumstances of life.

Now, even if my appraisal of the compelling nature of this argument is accurate, I grant that you are rational in your belief that an instance of evil is gratuitous if you look carefully but cannot see a greater good that has come from it, or a greater evil that has been prevented by it. That is a significant concession, but don't make too much of it. To return to a point made earlier in this book, it is possible to be rational in a belief that is false.[10] I will argue that this is the case.

DISTINCTIONS THAT MAKE A DIFFERENCE

Does gratuitous evil exist? I admit that some evil appears to be gratuitous, and that some evil is gratuitous in a qualified sense, but I deny the existence of evil that is categorically gratuitous. Let me explain.

When evil appears to be gratuitous but is not. Evil often seems to be gratuitous. Something bad happens, and in its aftermath we cannot see a greater good that has come or a greater evil that has been prevented. It is gratuitous as far as we can see. What seems to be gratuitous, however, may turn out not to be. Later developments may require a revision of an earlier conclusion. For Christians, there is no greater example of this than the crucifixion of Jesus. For three days following that horrific event, those who knew about it and cared would have been rational in their belief that it was gratuitous. It was senseless, pointless evil. The resurrection and all that followed in its wake were new developments that required a rethinking of their initial assessment.

Or consider the imprisonment of Nelson Mandela under the policy of institutional racism in South Africa. For twenty-seven years, his freedom was unjustly taken from him, and he endured other injustices during his incarceration. For twenty-seven years his followers would have been rational in their belief that this was gratuitous evil. But the story did not end there. There were ways in which Mandela was prepared by his prison experience to lead a nation-changing movement, and there were developments in the social and political world of South Africa that made that movement possible. His eventual release, leadership, and strategic role in ending apartheid brought greater goods that would not, as far as we know, have come about apart from his unjust captivity.

In its opening clause, the first premise of this argument posits a God who is omnipotent and good: "If a good, all-powerful God exists, then no gratuitous evil exists." If you grant this provisionally in the first premise, it has implications for evaluating the second premise that gratuitous evil exists. If we live in a world created and governed by a such a God, Christians say, evil may appear to be gratuitous because:

- The evil is physical and the greater good that comes from it, or the greater evil that is prevented, is spiritual.

- The greater good that comes from it, or the greater evil that is prevented, is for someone other than the one who suffered the evil (that is, it is redemptive in nature).

- The greater good that comes from it, or the greater evil that is prevented, occurs (or is prevented) in another place and another time.

- The greater good that comes from it, or the greater evil that is prevented, will be in an afterlife.

This is not special pleading. It just is the nature of the case, if, for the sake of argument, you grant that a Christian vision of the world is true.[11] Evil may seem gratuitous, but that does not make it so.[12]

When gratuitous evil exists in a qualified sense. Some evil is gratuitous because the greater good that is possible in a situation is contingent upon the actions of morally free agents that do not happen.[13] Suppose that Fred Wilson steals $100 from Stephanie Smith after she leaves an Automated Teller Machine, and that God permitted this to happen.

Greater goods that could come in consequence of this evil include the following:

- Mr. Wilson will be overcome with guilt, confess his crime, and become a model citizen who is known for good deeds to people in need.

- Ms. Smith will re-think her values and the inordinate status she has given to money, with an appropriate change of heart and a commitment to a simpler lifestyle.

39

- Ms. Smith will trust God with her finances from that point forward.

- Jennifer Matson, who witnessed the theft, will be moved to give Ms. Smith $100, and the two women will strike up a friendship that enriches both.

It is possible that none of these greater goods will come about because they are contingent upon the actions of morally free agents that do not occur. If so, gratuitous evil of a qualified sort results. An omnipotent God cannot eliminate such a state of affairs without also revoking the gift of moral freedom that makes it possible. A good God would not.

This is also true if the evil in question is not the act of a moral agent, but the result of natural forces. Let's say that Ms. Smith loses her house in a flood, and that the greater goods that could come from this include the following:

- Ms. Smith will move to another town where flooding is less likely, and will regard her new situation as a significant improvement.

- The local community will rally behind Ms. Smith, help her rebuild her house, and meet her physical and financial needs until life returns to normal.

- Ms. Smith, who previously had only a nominal belief in God, will come to believe that a relationship with God is of greater value than material possessions.

- Debbie Johnson, who reads about Ms. Smith's plight in the local newspaper, will volunteer to take care of the Smith children for the next month, and the two women will become friends for the rest of their lives.

It may be that none of these greater goods will come about because they are contingent upon actions of morally free agents that do not take place. In this case, again, gratuitous evil of a qualified sort results. An omnipotent God cannot eliminate such a state of affairs without also revoking the gift of moral freedom that makes it possible. A good God would not.

When morally free agents are involved, the critical issue is not whether a greater good resulted from an evil, or a greater evil was prevented (though both outcomes are possible), but whether a world in which there is moral freedom and the possibility of evil is better than a world without moral freedom. Christians say that it is, and that this is a morally sufficient reason for a good God to permit evil.[14]

Categorically gratuitous evil. I concede that gratuitous evil exists in appearance and in a contingent relationship with human freedom. I deny the existence of categorically gratuitous evil. If this sort of evil existed, its gratuitous nature would be simple, unqualified, and absolute. It would not serve a greater good or prevent a greater evil in any logically possible world in which it exists. (While the moral agents in our two stories did not bring about a greater good, there are logically possible worlds in which they do, which is another way of saying that they could have done otherwise).[15] We can give this evil a name and a definition, but it does not exist in our world.

Evil may appear to be gratuitous because we aren't in a position to see a greater good that has or will come from it or a greater evil that has been or will be prevented. It may be contingently gratuitous because it is related to God's gift of moral freedom. Categorically gratuitous evil, however, does not exist. The evil may be painfully real, but its unqualified gratuitous character is not. We can imagine it, but there is no such thing. Critics may assert that it exists and even protest loudly that it does. As we will see below, however, their arguments do not make good on their claims.

Before we get to those arguments, let's take a brief pause. If you disagree with me, it raises a very important question: Who is qualified to settle our disagreement? Who is in a position to determine when the standard of a morally sufficient reason has been met, or when it has not? Who is qualified to know if it will be met in the future or never will be? It would have to be someone with exhaustive and infallible knowledge of what constitutes a greater good or a greater evil in every instance in which evil occurs. It would have to be someone with complete and perfect knowledge of our world, including all morally free agents, from their first breath to their last, and whatever existence they may have in an afterlife. It would have to be someone with unlimited and unerring knowledge of all logically possible worlds, including all possible greater goods and evils that could come about from, or be prevented by, the existence of evil in our world.

Sounds like a task for an omniscient being.[16]

Either the set of omniscient beings has no members, if atheists are right, or it has one member, if Christians and other monotheists are right. If atheists are right, no one knows whether an evil in the past or the present will result in a greater good or the prevention of a greater evil in the future. We are left with a rhetorical contest without resolution. If Christians (and other monotheists) are right, the only one who knows these things and can render an infallible judgment on them is the God who created the world and permits evil in it.[17]

TWO ARGUMENTS

In conclusion, let's look at two versions of the argument from gratuitous evil. We have already seen the stronger of the two:

(1) If a good, all-powerful God exists, gratuitous evil does not exist.
(2) Gratuitous evil exists.
(3) Therefore, a good, all-powerful God does not exist.

SECOND DEFENSE: DIVINE GOODNESS

Atheists claim that there is gratuitous evil in the world and insist that believers must prove otherwise. I object. The burden of proof lies with the proponents of the argument. Since it is their claim that gratuitous evil exists, they must demonstrate that it does. I don't believe that they can.

First, their claim requires a leap that logic cannot make. There is a hidden premise in their assertion. It becomes apparent when we recall that evil is gratuitous if there is no morally sufficient reason for its existence. If E is an instance of evil, this is the tacit premise: "We can't see a morally sufficient reason for E." This is the inference drawn from it: "There are no morally sufficient reasons for E." The inference is a *non sequitur*. It does not logically follow. It does not follow from the fact that we cannot see something that it does not exist.[18] That I cannot see you as I write this implies nothing about your existence. That you cannot see me implies nothing about mine.

Second, saying that one cannot see something is not a statement of positive evidence, but an admission of ignorance. Atheists may be faulted for claiming to know more than they do; they should not be blamed for not knowing what they cannot know. They are not in a position to say that any instance of evil in the world is, in fact, gratuitous, and there is nothing they can do to change that. It is the human situation.[19] Our epistemic limitations are too great, our knowledge, too scant.

Perhaps a more modest version of the argument will succeed:

(1) If a good, all-powerful God exists, gratuitous evil does not exist.
(2) Gratuitous evil probably exists.
(3) Therefore, a good, all-powerful God probably does not exist.

Claiming a probable rather than an actual state of affairs in the second premise and the conclusion may seem to make the argument more reasonable and tenable. In fact, however, it fails on those very terms.

First, it still involves a *non sequitur*. If we say again that E is an instance of evil, there is a chasm in the logic between "We can't see a morally sufficient reason for *E*." and "There probably are no morally sufficient reasons for *E*." One does not follow from the other. The fact that we cannot see something tells us nothing about the probability of its existence. From the mere fact that I cannot see a solution to a physics problem, nothing can be inferred about the probability that a solution exists.[20] From the fact that I cannot see the Northern Lights from my home in Colorado, nothing can be inferred about the likelihood that there is such a polar light display.

Second, we still don't know enough. If we are not in a position to see future goods that may come or future evils that may be averted in consequence of a past or present evil, we cannot establish probability in the matter. Suppose that we watch two runners in a ten-mile race crest a hill at the quarter-mile mark and disappear from our sight. There isn't any way to know which runner will win the race, or even which runner will probably win. We are not in a position to know, and there is nothing more that we can say about it. You might cheer Runner A, and I, Runner B. You may have reasons for believing that your runner will win; I may have reasons for believing that mine will prevail. You might say, "My runner was faster to the top of that hill!" I might respond, "Yes, but have you never heard the story of the tortoise and the hare? They still have most of the race to go." The only one who knows the outcome is someone standing at the finish line, and that isn't either of us. So it is when we are asked to evaluate the status of something – in this case whether an instance of evil is gratuitous or not – when that status can only be determined by unknown states of affairs in the future.

Third, there isn't an objective way to determine whose claim of probability has won and whose has been defeated. If we were using a statistical notion of probability, an outcome could be measured. In principle we might come to an agreement. In this argument, however, both sides must appeal to a qualitative property of likelihood in a comparison of rival points of view. There isn't a way to measure this.

Fourth, because we are dealing with a qualitative notion, subjective factors come into play. There is great value in discussion and debate. You might convince me that your argument is stronger; I might persuade you of the strength of mine. We might both come away with greater clarity in our thinking. At the end of the day, however, there isn't an objective, neutral position from which the probability of our points of view can be judged.

Finally, this argument is either unpersuasive or it commits the fallacy of ambiguity, and so fails. The second premise and the conclusion use the word "probably." For the argument to succeed, the word must have the same meaning in both instances. In the second premise, the critic says, in effect, that he cannot see a greater good that has come from an instance of suffering, or a greater evil that has been averted, and so concludes that the evil in question is probably gratuitous. We might call this *as-far-as-we-can-see* probability. Now, if this meaning is also used in the conclusion – *As far as we can see,* a good, all-powerful God probably does not exist – the argument may tell us something about our limited vantage point, but it says nothing convincing about the probable existence or non-existence of God.

Now consider the conclusion of the argument. The probability of the existence of God cannot be decided on the basis of any single issue, including evil. The broadest possible range of evidence must be taken into account. Let's call this *all-things-considered* probability. This is a different notion than we began the argument with. If critics import this meaning of probability into the conclusion to give it greater strength, they commit the fallacy of ambiguity, and the argument fails.

CONCLUDING ARGUMENT

With the understanding that I am referring to evil that is categorically gratuitous, let me conclude with my own argument:

    (1) If a good, all-powerful God exists, gratuitous evil does not exist.
    (2) A good, all-powerful God exists;
    (3) Therefore, gratuitous evil does not exist.[21]

The strength of this argument depends on the strength of the premise that a good, all-powerful God exists. Such a God would not permit such evil (which is implied in the first premise). Even if I don't know why God permits one evil or another, there are good reasons for believing in God, who does know.[22] This is not an arbitrary move. It arises suitably from a humble recognition that an omniscient God knows things that we don't, and a confidence that we are on sturdy ground in affirming that an omniscient, good, all-powerful God exists. Even if logical certainty is beyond our reach (and it is), and we acknowledge subjective factors in our beliefs (and we must), this is where the issue must be decided.[23]

POSTSCRIPT: GRATUITOUS EVIL AND THE CROSS

How odd that an instrument of torture and death should become the centerpiece of worship and faith for nearly two and a half billion people around the world today! Yet it is true. The instrument is a cross, the one who hung upon it was Jesus of Nazareth, and the billions who embrace this in faith are Christians.

The cross is an invitation to rethink our understanding of God. John Stott captured its significance in these words:

> I could never myself believe in God, if it were not for the cross. The only God I believe in is the One Nietzsche ridiculed as 'God on the cross.' In the real world of pain, how could one worship a God who was immune to it? I have entered many Buddhist temples in different Asian countries and stood respectfully before the statue of the Buddha, his legs crossed, arms folded, eyes closed, the ghost of a smile playing round his mouth, a remote look on his face, detached from the agonies of the world. But each time after a while I have had to turn away. And in imagination I have turned instead to that lonely, twisted, tortured figure on the cross, nails through hands and feet, back lacerated, limbs wrenched, brow bleeding from thorn-pricks, mouth dry and intolerably thirsty, plunged in Godforsaken darkness. That is the God for me![24]

The startling claim of Christians is that in Jesus the God who created and sustains the universe has drawn near to us, so near that he became one of us. The God who governs history is so intimately involved in human life that he made it his own. If that were not enough, the more astonishing claim is that in Jesus God submitted himself fully to the conditions of our humanity, lived without wrongdoing, and then, on a cross, offered his sinless life as full payment for the sins of the world.

> Have this mind among yourselves, which is yours in Christ Jesus, who, though he was in the form of God, did not count equality with God a thing to be grasped, but emptied himself, by taking the form of a servant, being born in the likeness of men. And being found in human form, he humbled himself by becoming obedient to the point of death, even death on a cross. (Philippians 2:5-8)

> God shows his love for us in that while we were still sinners, Christ died for us. (Romans 5:8)

> In Christ God was reconciling the world to himself. (2 Corinthians 5:19)

The cross is also an invitation to see evil differently.[25] There is no way to euphemize it: Death by crucifixion is horrendous evil. In the case of Christ, however, it was also redemptive, because God was in Christ, on the cross, reconciling the world to himself. In a powerful paradox, great evil has brought great good. What destroyed now saves. What brought death now brings life. What seemed senseless turns out to be the most significant thing that has happened in the world.

We are invited to see our troubled world in light of the cross. Suffering, pain, and evil may seem pointless, but they are not what they seem, or need not be, because they point to what God has done for us in Christ. And that changes everything.

QUESTIONS FOR THOUGHT AND DISCUSSION

1. "A morally sufficient reason for permitting evil includes bringing about a greater good that would not otherwise happen, or preventing a greater evil that otherwise would." What do you think of this principle? Can you think of examples of each?

2. Discuss the author's understanding of apparent and contingent gratuitous evil. Is it convincing?

3. Discuss the author's understanding of categorically gratuitous evil. Is it convincing?

4. What do you think of the three versions of arguments on gratuitous evil and God? Which argument to you agree with, and why?

5. Discuss the Postscript on the Cross and Gratuitous Evil. Do you agree or disagree? Why?

CHAPTER 4

THIS WORLD AND THE NEXT
A THEODICY

There is good reason to believe that gratuitous evil does not exist in our world, not only because we sometimes see a greater good that would not otherwise happen, and sometimes become aware of a greater evil that has been prevented, but because there are good reasons to believe in a good, all-powerful God who would not allow it.[1]

A world designed for morally free creatures is better than a world without them. If God were to prevent all natural evil so that there was no possibility of sickness or calamity, it would also eliminate many acts of kindness, compassion, cooperation, generosity, courage, and heroism – all of which are grounded in moral freedom. If God were to remove our freedom in order to eliminate the possibility of moral evil, it would also remove the possibility of joy and the good life he intends for us. Neither of these possible worlds would be a better world, and that is a morally sufficient reason for God's permission of evil in ours.[2]

In this chapter we will explore morally sufficient reasons for God's permission of evil in his world. This is sometimes called a *theodicy*, or an attempt to vindicate God and his ways.[3] I offer this with hesitation, first, because I cannot imagine God asking me to defend him. It would be like the sun asking a candle to help illumine the earth, or a hurricane asking a handheld fan to help blow water across the sea. I hesitate, secondly, because I know so little. There is much that is a mystery to me. I am mindful of words like these:

> For my thoughts are not your thoughts,
>   neither are your ways my ways, declares the LORD.
> For as the heavens are higher than the earth,
>   so are my ways higher than your ways
>   and my thoughts than your thoughts. (Isaiah 55:8-9)

> O, the depth of the riches and wisdom and knowledge of God!
>   How unsearchable are his judgments and how inscrutable his ways!
> "For who has known the mind of the Lord, or who has been his
>   counselor?" (Romans 11:33-34)

I know less of the wisdom and knowledge of God than a tiny crustacean on an ocean floor knows of a ship on the surface miles above. You might think that such a confession would (or should) mark an early end to this chapter. One of the central affirmations of Christian faith, however, is that God has revealed truth about himself and his ways. He has disclosed what would otherwise be closed to us. Not enough or clearly enough to satisfy our curiosity, but enough to help us navigate our way through life with joy.[4] My offering is a reflection upon what God has made known in the Scriptures he has given.

QUESTIONS OF VALUE

The problem of evil has led us to notions of greater good and greater evil. Much of the disagreement between believers and their critics lies here.

Whether you agree with them or not, these judgments of value are essential to a Christian vision of life:

- A virtuous character is a greater good than freedom from suffering and pain.

- A misshapen character is a greater evil than suffering and pain.

- An eternal good is a greater good than freedom from temporal suffering and pain.

- Eternal suffering and pain are greater evils than temporal suffering and pain.

- The undimmed, unending enjoyment of God in heaven is an immeasurably greater good than any temporal suffering and pain on the earth.

If you start here, Christians say, the world begins to make sense. If you don't, it never will.

GREATER EVILS

A Misshapen Character. I understand that what I am about to say is so far removed from the values of our culture that it will seem preposterous to many. Nevertheless, Christians believe that God permits and uses pain in our lives because one of its possibilities (possible because our morally free response is required) is averting the greater evil of a misshapen character.[5]

C.S. Lewis put this way:

> The human spirit will not even begin to try to surrender self will as long as all seems to be well with it. Now error and sin both have

this property, that the deeper they are the less their victim suspects their existence; they are masked evil. Pain is unmasked, unmistakable evil; every man knows that something is wrong when he is being hurt . . . . pain is not only immediately recognisable evil, but evil impossible to ignore. We can rest contentedly in our sins and in our stupidities; and anyone who has watched gluttons shovelling down the most exquisite foods as if they did not know what they were eating, will admit that we can ignore even pleasure. But pain insists upon being attended to. God whispers to us in our pleasures, speaks in our conscience, but shouts in our pains: it is His megaphone to rouse a deaf world.[6]

Even if we do not, God takes the development of our character seriously. He permits and uses pain and suffering in our lives because he knows that if he does not rouse us with such a warning we will live comfortably in our sin until we are in a hellish place where we cannot do otherwise.[7]

Hell.[8]   Pleasure in God is our greatest good. There is nothing better for us. The pure, undimmed, and unbroken enjoyment of God is another way of describing heaven. The pain of separation and alienation from God is our greatest evil, whether we experience it as disquietude, despondence, depression, or despair, or it is the ultimate, unending sorrow of those who reject God, which is what we mean by hell.[9]

If pleasure is an invitation to something far greater, pain is a warning of something far worse. Temporal pleasures point to the goodness of the Creator and beckon us to draw near, where we will discover "fullness of joy" and "pleasures forevermore."[10] Temporal pain and suffering point to the brokenness of a world in rebellion against God, and warn us of the dire, eternal consequences of continuing in that state. God does not wish that for anyone, and will take extreme measures, if necessary, to keep them from it.[11]

GREATER GOODS

The glory of God. In the largest possible frame of reference, Christians say that everything in the universe is teleologically related to the glory of God.[12] His glory is displayed in his creative wisdom and power, from quarks to black holes, from protons and photons to galaxies beyond our count. It is disclosed in his goodness, in the creation of a world that is beneficial to us, that meets our needs and fulfills our desires. His glory is revealed in his justice when he punishes evil or comes to the aid of its victims.[13] It is shown in his mercy when he withholds punishment from those who deserve it, and in his grace when he is generous to the undeserving.

Even if we don't know how something might serve the glory of God, believers say that God's glory is the Greater Good in everything that happens, and say, further, that our joy (which is a greater good for us) is fullest when we embrace this. This is true even when we go through ordeals in life. It is a fruitful paradox, and joy is its fruit. Believers don't expect those who do not live out this paradox to understand or appreciate it, but we would not trade this greater good, this joy, for health, wealth, or the applause of many.

The good life. God's glory and our joy are linked because glory and joy are united in God and he offers himself to us. Karl Barth wrote:

> God's glory is the indwelling joy of His divine being which as such shines out from Him, which overflows in its richness, which in its super-abundance . . . communicates itself.

> God's glory is His overflowing self-communicating joy. By its very nature it is that which gives joy.

> But we cannot overlook the fact that God is glorious in such a way that He radiates joy.[14]

We are invited into a fellowship of this glory and this joy. This is the good life. This is the greater good that God is pursuing for us. He takes action to bring us into a relationship with him and to transform us so that we become the kind of people who seek his glory and joy, and who, in their seeking and finding, flourish in life. This is the morally sufficient reason behind God's permission of evil. It is the "complex good" that God seeks to bring from the "simple evil" of human rebellion and consequent suffering.[15] To the extent that we can fathom his purposes, this is what God is up to in the ordeals of life.

Soul-making. God's joy and his moral perfections are united in an eternal, unbreakable bond. He delights in his righteousness, rejoices in his justice, and takes pleasure in his steadfast love.[16] Our joy is linked to this as his image-bearers. As our character reflects his, God shares his joy with us (or, put another way, we enter into his joy).[17] In the first chapter of the human story this reflection and sharing were perfect, unbroken, and effortless. Not so in our chapter. We participate in God's joy only as he renews his moral likeness in us.[18] For that to happen, sin must be forgiven, a relationship must be restored, hearts must be transformed, and lives must be changed. This is what God offers and accomplishes in redemption.[19]

When God's purposes of redemption are fully realized there will be "new heavens and a new earth in which righteousness dwells."[20] Short of that, and in preparation for that world, joy demands a "soul-making" environment.[21] It requires a habitat in which there can be growth in virtue. It mandates a world in which there are moral heroes – men and women whose character has been forged in the fire of life's challenges – and others who seek to be like them. Short of joy's consummation in the world to come, a world in which joy is our greatest good will feature challenges to meet, obstacles to move, opportunities to seize, possibilities to pursue, risks to take, dangers to embrace, and fears to defeat. It will champion courage, compassion, sacrifice, generosity, resilience, and resolve. Jesus and his followers believed that they lived in such a world. If we are clear-sighted, it looks very much like ours.

The moral freedom that makes joy possible is most significant (that is, we are most virtuous in our exercise of God's gift of moral freedom) when the stakes are high and the risks are great.[22] The stakes are highest and the risks seem greatest when the signs of God's presence and the evidence of his handiwork curl into question marks.[23] Whether we like it or not, God draws near and sometimes he withdraws. He discloses and sometimes conceals. He shouts and sometimes whispers. Sometimes he points without a whisper. Sometimes he doesn't even point. Sometimes he waits for us to cry out to him.

> Yes, if you cry out for insight
>   and raise your voice for understanding;
> if you seek it like silver
>   and search for it as for hidden treasures;
> then you will understand the fear of the LORD
>   and find the knowledge of God. (Proverbs 2:3-5, RSV)

Joy comes when, in the freedom he has granted us, we say "Yes" to God, even when the stakes are high, the peril is great, and the path before us seems uncertain. This is never truer than when we face suffering and pain and encounter evil in the world:

> More than that, we rejoice in our sufferings, knowing that suffering produces endurance. (Romans 5:3, RSV)

> You joyfully accepted the plundering of your property, since you knew that you yourselves had a better possession and an abiding one. (Hebrews 10:34, RSV)

> Count it all joy, my brothers, when you meet trials of various kinds, for you know that the testing of your faith produces steadfastness. (James 1:2-3, RSV)

In the crucible of life's ordeals, hearts are formed and joy is refined. In a fallen world, joy requires this. Joy mandates a world in which character-quests are possible and we become the kind of people who embrace them. You might wish for a different world, or to be exempt from God's soul-shaping purposes for this one, but neither is an option he has given us.

AN ETERNAL GOOD

Living in light of eternity. Although many in our day seem to have forgotten, Christians through the ages have believed and taught that we begin to make sense of this life only as we see it in light of eternity. God's plans for us include this life, and stretch beyond it for ages without end. It would be a mistake to call that an *afterlife*. If anything, ours now is a *pre-life*. It is preparation for Real Life, which is yet to come. Jesus used the word *joy* to describe it: "Well done, good and faithful servant. . . . Enter into the joy of your master." [24] The apostle Paul used the word *glory*: "For this light momentary affliction is preparing for us an eternal weight of glory beyond all comparison." [25]

Imagine a great set of balanced scales. If we could put all the pain, suffering, and evil in the history of the world on one side, and the glory and joy of a single moment in heaven on the other, the scale would break under the weight of glory and joy, and the ground beneath would shudder and sink into oblivion. The glory and joy of heaven are incommensurable goods. [26] They are so great that nothing in our world can measure them. No model can compare them. No computer can calculate them. No lab can assess them. In our world we know their smallest part in traces of glory and moments of joy.

The best is yet to come! In the early 18th century, philosopher and mathematician, Gottfried Leibnitz, crafted a response to the problem of evil centered on the idea of the "best of all possible worlds." His argument was not that this is a perfect world (which is refuted by cursory observation), but that of all the worlds God could have created, this world, with its balance of good and evil, is the best of them.[27]

Apart from problems with the notion of the best of all possible worlds, the belief that our world has that status does not fit the eschatological focus in the teaching of Jesus and his early followers.[28] For them, the best is yet to come. This eschatological orientation can be seen in the relationship between joy and hope in the Christian Scriptures. They are thread and strand in the weave of a Godward life.[29] The apostle Paul put it this way in a prayer: "May the God of *hope* fill you with all *joy* and peace in believing, so that by the power of the Holy Spirit you may abound in *hope*."[30] Joy is drawn to the future.[31] It longs to find its fulfillment in the ultimate realization of God's purposes, when his Kingdom comes and his will is done on earth as it is in heaven.[32] This is hope's joy. This is joy's hope.

Hope embraces the *already* and *not-yet* dimensions of joy because both are true to the nature of God's Kingdom, joy's native environment. Because it is true to the Kingdom, however, there is more to joy than present and future tenses. Joy in our present experience, even in our suffering and pain, is the joy of the future Kingdom penetrating the present in advance of its final consummation.[33] It "rends indeed the very web" of history and "lets a gleam come through."[34] It is a foretaste of the new heavens and the new earth. An installment. The first fruits of our future joy in God's undimmed presence. Joy is the closest thing to heaven that we can know in our present state, because it is a bit of heaven itself. It is a brand from heaven's fire. A spark from heaven's blazing glory. A breath of heaven's air. A fragrance from its orchards. A bar of its music. A beam of its light cast into the shadows of our world.

This is not the best of all possible worlds. It is related to the best world, which is yet to come, as a chrysalis is related to a butterfly. One is gloriously transformed into the other. This eschatological good, anticipated in experiences of joy, is the ultimate morally sufficient reason for God creating moral agents who can choose good and evil, and who have chosen evil and brought pain and suffering into our world.

POSTSCRIPT: FINDING JOY IN THE ORDEALS OF LIFE

In this final section we will leave philosophical debates behind and re-enter the world of personal experience. This is my response to what I referred to at the outset as the existential or emotional problem of evil.

We might wish that it were otherwise, but God doesn't offer answers to all of our questions. He offers himself to us in our questions. He doesn't offer life without suffering and pain. In a powerful paradox, he offers joy that comes in and through these things. It is an offer with conditions. There is nothing artificial or arbitrary about this. C.S. Lewis wrote:

> Good things as well as bad, you know, are caught by a kind of infection. If you want to get warm you must stand near the fire: if you want to be wet you must get into the water. If you want joy, power, peace, eternal life, you must get close to, or even into, the thing that has them. They are not a sort of prize which God could, if He chose, just hand out to anyone. They are a great fountain of energy and beauty spurting up at the very centre of reality. If you are close to it, the spray will wet you: if you are not, you will remain dry.[35]

Because joy is a connection with God, it is possible only as we get close to him. We position ourselves for joy, even in times of suffering and pain, when we draw near to God.

There are three kinds of nearness for us to consider. The first is the nearness of measurable space. If two things are close to each other in this way, the distance between them is small. The smaller the space, the nearer they are. Because God is *omnipresent*, he is always near in this way. The apostle Paul told his audience in Athens that God is never far from us, for "in him we live and move and have our being."[36] As you read these words, God is to your right and to your left. He is above you, below you, before you, and behind. God not only surrounds you at all times, he is nearer to you than the breath in your lungs, the blood in your veins, the thoughts of your mind, and the affections of your heart. In Augustine's words: God is "more intimately present to me than my innermost being."[37]

We may be unaware of his presence, but we can never be nearer to God in the events and situations of our lives than we already are, because he is everywhere present at the same time. There is no escaping God's presence,[38] but we can ignore it. We can be out of touch with it. We can miss it. The awareness of his presence begins in meditation, as we focus our thoughts and affections on this life-shaping truth.[39] There is comfort, strength, peace, and joy as we cultivate an awareness of God's presence with us. We can keep the Lord always before us. Always at our right hand.[40] Always in our "mind's eye."[41] Like a radio that has been tuned to receive unseen sound waves that surround us at all times (even if we are unaware of them), our hearts can be tuned to God's company and the music of his presence.

Spatial nearness is one thing; relational nearness is another. Two people sitting next to each other on a crowded city bus might be close in the first sense (measurable space) but far from each other in this second sense (relational proximity). They might not know each other at all. When we talk about "close friends," this is the nearness we have in mind. It isn't possible to be nearer or farther from God in the first sense, but it is possible to be near or far from God in this way:

> The LORD says: 'These people come near to me with their mouth and honor me with their lips, but their hearts are far from me. (Isaiah 29:13, NIV)

> The LORD is near to the brokenhearted. (Psalm 34:18)

> The haughty he knows from afar. (Psalm 138:6)

> Draw near to God, and he will draw near to you. (James 4:8)

This nearness to God is a nearness of hearts. It is a relational closeness that comes from common interests and concerns. It is an intimacy that comes from sharing life. This is what the Psalmist had in mind when he wrote, "For me it is good to be near God."[42]

Relational nearness to God is a cultivated way of living in the world. It is a congeniality of hearts. It is a nearness that is nurtured and grows when our hearts are aligned with God's, when he is often in our thoughts and treasured in our affections, when our wills beat in rhythm with his. Habituate your thoughts here. Make it a Godward focus in prayer, and then begin acting in appropriate, fitting ways. (The Bible calls this "walking in the truth."[43]) There is joy here, even in times of suffering and pain.

The third kind of nearness I would call the nearness of similitude or likeness. If a painter captures a landscape on a canvas, we say that the painting is "close" to the original. It is near to it in its likeness. We were created in the image of God. In our fallenness, sin has sullied and distorted that likeness. God's image is restored in us in redemption as the Spirit of God re-shapes our hearts so that we become more like Christ.[44] If we draw near to God in times of suffering and pain, he uses these things, as a Potter uses clay, water, and a turning wheel, to make us more like his Son. Little by little in a life-long process, his character is mirrored in ours. His way of living in the world becomes ours.

Jesus is the self-portrait of God in human form. He is the perfect image of God in humanity.[45] The more like him we become, the closer to God we will be, the greater our joy even as we go through ordeals of suffering and pain. "That my joy may be in you," Jesus said, "that your joy may be full."[46]

QUESTIONS FOR THOUGHT AND DISCUSSION

1. Looking at the list of value judgments about greater evils and greater goods, do you agree with them? What difference does this make for the problem of evil?

2. What do you think of the author's understanding of heaven and hell? (See also endnote 8.) Do you agree? Disagree?

3. What do you think about the author's treatment of God's glory and our joy?

4. Do you agree or disagree with the author about this world as a "soul-making environment?" What difference does this make for the problem of evil?

5. What are the three types of nearness to God, and how are they relevant to joy?

CHAPTER 5

JOY AND
THE KINGDOM OF GOD

THE WORLD'S TRAVAIL

At the end of the day evil is not an intellectual problem to be solved, but a destructive force that must be overcome.[1] God permits evil in his sovereign purposes for our world, but he regards it as a usurper that must be removed, and an enemy that must be banished from his realm. Much of this he intends to do through us.

Sadly, many who should believe this don't seem to. The very people you would expect to find venturing into the world to make it a better place are preoccupied with other things. Lesser things. It is not that they have forsaken the world in a religious sense; they have chosen to neglect the world, to become obsessed with personal interests and concerns, which they dress in religious garb. Hard words, but too often true.[2]

Joy is the highest and best pleasure we can know. My one fear in writing about this is that the cultural hermeneutic of the day will see joy as a subjective experience to be sought in a private inner sanctum isolated from and irrelevant to the world and its travail.[3] That would be a mistake of enormous proportions! Archbishop Temple said it well: "Christian joy and hope do not arise from an ignoring of the evil in the world, but from facing it at its worst."[4]

Joy cannot be divorced from the kind of people we are becoming in our pursuit of moral excellence. It cannot be separated from our call to live lovingly, justly, and responsibly in God's world. Those who think that they can flee the world and its problems to gain joy will be disappointed, because it cannot be found that way. Joy is not a grail whose quest takes us away from a world in need; it is more like a magnetic force that draws us into its plight.[5]

Joy does not look away from suffering in the world.[6] It faces it head-on, without flinching, and then looks through it. Suffering is not entirely opaque. There is much that we cannot see, but we can see enough for joy. Joy looks through the lens of suffering to see what God is seeking to do, and exults in this:

> More than that, we rejoice in our sufferings, knowing that suffering produces endurance. (Romans 5:3, RSV)

> You joyfully accepted the plundering of your property, since you knew that you yourselves had a better possession and an abiding one. (Hebrews 10:34, RSV)

> Count it all joy, my brothers, when you meet trials of various kinds, for you know that the testing of your faith produces steadfastness. (James 1:2-3, RSV)

Joy is ruthlessly realistic about the world we live in, but refuses to reach the same conclusions drawn by pessimists and fatalists. Because joy is illumined by a Light they do not have, it envisions possibilities for the world that they do not see and cannot entertain.

JESUS ON THE KINGDOM OF GOD

What is God doing to defeat evil in his world? We see a glimpse of this in what Jesus and his early followers said about the Kingdom of God.

When Jesus began his public ministry, he stirred the air with the dramatic announcement: "The time has come; the kingdom of God is upon you; repent and believe in the gospel."[7] A new era dawned with the coming of the Christ. A new epoch began. History skidded around this turning point and moved in a new direction.

Ancient prophecies sprang to life on the lips of Jesus:

> The Spirit of the Lord is upon me,
>> because he has anointed me
>> to preach good news to the poor.
> He has sent me to proclaim release to the captives
>> and recovering of sight to the blind,
>> to set at liberty those who are oppressed,
> to proclaim the acceptable year of the Lord. (Luke 4:18-21)[8]

In the words and deeds of Jesus the Supernatural and natural realms met. In that meeting lives were transformed, wounded hearts were mended, and broken bodies were healed. It was an incursion of the Kingdom of God. Yet to be acknowledged, the rightful King was staking his claim.

Jesus taught his followers to make this Kingdom prayer centermost in the way they lived in the world:

> Our Father in heaven,
>> hallowed be your name.
> *Your kingdom come,*
>> *your will be done,*
>> *on earth as it is in heaven.*

Give us this day our daily bread,
   and forgive us our debts,
    as we also have forgiven our debtors.
And lead us not into temptation,
   but deliver us from evil.
For yours is the Kingdom, the power and glory, forever. Amen.
(Matthew 6:9-13)[9]

When Jesus preached it was to proclaim the Kingdom.[10] When he taught it was to expound the Kingdom.[11] When he spoke in parables it was to illustrate the Kingdom.[12] When he cast out demons it was warfare for the Kingdom.[13] When he healed it was to display the power of the Kingdom.[14] When he dispatched his disciples throughout the land, it was as emissaries of the Kingdom.[15] When he commissioned them before his departure, it was to take the Gospel of the Kingdom to the ends of the earth.[16] When he promised to build the Church, he gave it the authority of the Kingdom.[17] In the forty days between his resurrection and his ascension he spoke with his disciples about the Kingdom of God.[18]

What is the Kingdom of God? As Jesus and early Christians saw it, it is the dynamic reign of God breaking into history, bringing righteousness, peace, and joy – the boon of his empire.[19] Its fullness lies in the future.[20] One day "every knee will bow, and every tongue will confess that Jesus Christ is Lord, to the glory of God the Father."[21] When that happens, no one will pray for the Kingdom to come, for it will surround us on every side and govern all of life.

The Gospel of the Kingdom is a declaration that the Kingdom of God has entered the world in the life, death, and resurrection of Jesus Christ.[22] It has arrived in advance of its final realization, conquering evil, bringing forgiveness of sin and reconciliation with God, restoring relationships, healing brokenness and disease, and bestowing the blessings of God's reign.[23] It transforms people who will change the world.

ENTERING THE KINGDOM

The Kingdom of God isn't a place, but we must still enter it.[24] Jesus said so, and he knows better than anyone. The gateway to the Kingdom is repentance and faith. Again, Jesus said so, and he should know: "Now after John was arrested, Jesus came into Galilee, proclaiming the gospel of God, and saying, 'The time is fulfilled, and the kingdom of God is at hand; repent and believe in the gospel.'"[25]

To enter the Kingdom we must cross a threshold. The first step is repentance: embracing radically different ways of thinking about God and ourselves.[26] We have falsely imagined God. We have believed that he is indifferent to our sin, and that he will indulge us in our sinfulness. In truth, he is altogether righteous and burns with a pure and wholesome hatred of all that is not. Because we have misunderstood God, we have also nurtured false views of ourselves. The ease with which we accommodate our wrongdoing leads us to believe that our condition is natural, normal, and acceptable. Not so! In the highest and fullest sense of the word, God is holy; in the starkest contrast imaginable, we are not. We are crooked. Bent. Polluted. Stained. Guilty. Worthy of condemnation. Repentance lets truth about God and our condition pierce our hearts with sorrow – not feeling sorry for ourselves, but lamenting the sin that is a monumental affront to God.

Our false understanding of God not only underestimates his righteousness and its unrelenting demands, it understates his boundless love and desire to bless. In our distorted vision, we see him as grudging, stinting, loath to part with his hoard. Our false god is utterly unlike God as Jesus understood him. The true God is like the father whose prodigal son returns in repentance, who sees his son from a distance, is moved with compassion, runs to embrace and kiss his boy, and celebrates his return with a music, dancing, and a great feast.[27]

In repentance we turn from sinful thoughts, affections, words, and deeds that alienate us from God and create a world filled with idols – false gods, every one. In faith, our second step into the Kingdom, we turn to the living and true God.[28] The bad news (for us) is that God is implacably hostile to all that is antithetical to his character and incompatible with his purposes. The good news (for us) is that his hostility is "not to the sinner but to the sin."[29] He loves sinners. He forgives repentant sinners. He welcomes them as friends. He invites them into a fellowship of love. He relates to them in grace and mercy, and gifts them with righteousness, peace, and unspeakable joy. This is the good news of the Kingdom. This is the favor of the King. Faith is the heart that is open and the hand that receives all that God is prepared to give.

Repentance and faith are the first steps into the Kingdom and then a way of living in the Kingdom.[30] They orient us to God and his purposes. They are relational dispositions, tuning our hearts to God's. They are transformative practices, breaking the power of sin and creating an inner environment in which the fruit of God's Spirit can grow.[31] They keep us humble with the recognition of our own fallenness and need, grateful for the gracious riches of God's love in Christ, and joyful in an undeserved life under God's beneficent reign.

AGENTS OF THE KINGDOM

If we respond to the invitation to live in the Kingdom and to act on its behalf, what does that mean in practical terms? The apostle Paul gives us a clue: "The kingdom of God is not food and drink but righteousness and peace and joy in the Holy Spirit,"[32] We are called to pursue righteousness, peace, and joy in the Holy Spirit. This is not embracing an ideology, advancing the agenda of a political party, or protecting or expanding the interests of a nation. God is not a partisan.[33] His Kingdom rules over all. It is meant for all. Righteousness, peace, and joy in the Holy Spirit are supernatural forces that can work in and through us to transform the world and bring the will of God to the earth as it now governs in heaven.

Righteousness, peace, and joy describe the culture of God's Kingdom. They shape the foreign and domestic policies of the Kingdom. They represent the Kingdom-in-action, empowered by God's Spirit. They are not what we hope to find when we look within; they are what we should expect to find when we see people living together – in the power of the Spirit – as representatives of God's Kingdom in the world. They are spheres of service, as Paul says next: "For the one who serves Christ in this is pleasing to God and approved by men."[34] People of the Kingdom are called to be agents of righteousness, brokers of peace, and catalysts of joy in the world. If they do this well, Christ is served, God is pleased, and those who receive the benefit of their action will respond with approval.

Righteousness in this context is "righteous action"[35] or what biblical writers referred to as "doing righteousness."[36] It is action taken to promote and protect the well-being of others.[37] The righteousness of the Kingdom is what the Psalmist thought of when he said of God, "Righteousness and justice are the foundation of his throne."[38] God is committed to a world in which his creatures truly thrive. Ancient people of faith often praised God for his commitment to those who were least likely to flourish in a fallen, sinful world. We practice the righteousness of the Kingdom when our hearts align with God's, and, on his behalf and in partnership with him we seek the good of others – especially those who need our help if they are to prosper in life:[39]

He executes justice for the fatherless and the widow,
and loves the sojourner, giving him food and clothing.
(Deuteronomy 10:18)

The LORD works righteousness
    and justice for all who are oppressed. (Psalm 103:6)

Happy is he whose help is the God of Jacob,
    whose hope is in the LORD his God,
    who made heaven and earth,
        the sea, and all that is in them;
    who keeps faith for ever;
        who executes justice for the oppressed;
    who gives food to the hungry.
The LORD sets the prisoners free;
    the LORD opens the eyes of the blind,
    the LORD lifts up those who are bowed down;
    the LORD loves the righteous.
The LORD watches over the sojourners,
    he upholds the widow and the fatherless;
    but the way of the wicked he brings to ruin.
The LORD will reign for ever,
    thy God, O Zion, to all generations.
Praise the LORD! (Psalm 146:5-10)[40]

Those who have been brought into a right relationship with God long to see others join them. They yearn to see others flourish in God's will.[41] They eagerly share with all whose hearts are open, but seek the oppressed, the hungry, the poor, the fettered, the crippled, the deaf, and the blind, because they know that God is committed to them and their plight. They long to see them discover their help in the God of Jacob and their hope in the LORD their God. They take great pleasure in joining God in what he is doing, becoming the voice through which he speaks and the hands with which he touches people in need. This is the righteousness of the Kingdom.[42] It must be important to followers of Jesus, because it was important to him.[43] He saw it as the heart of his mission, fulfilling Isaiah's prophetic words:

> The Spirit of the Lord is upon me,
>   because he has anointed me to preach good news to the poor.
> He has sent me to proclaim release to the captives
>   and recovering of sight to the blind,
> to set at liberty those who are oppressed,
>   to proclaim the acceptable year of the Lord. (Luke 4:18-19, RSV)[44]

What about Kingdom peace? It is tempting to see this as an experience of inner tranquility, but that moves us further from Paul's thought in this context. There are times when the apostle does have personal peace in mind.[45] Those who know this experience treasure it above all earthly possessions. There are times when he is thinking about peace between people. Sometimes it is peace between fellow believers.[46] Sometimes it includes all who enter the circle of our lives: "If possible, so far as it depends on you, live peaceably with all."[47] When peace is put into the context of God's Kingdom, however, its boundaries are as broad as his reign. It is global in its design and intent. It is a harmony in the world that emerges from right relationships – with God, our neighbor, and the created order in which we have been placed. Because they have been introduced to this peace, people of the Kingdom are peacemakers. They seek to resolve conflict, to end strife, and to guide others into relational health. Before a world that is always watching, they model the possibilities of flourishing in life together.

Kingdom peace is the fulfillment of what the prophets called *shalom*: life at its best under God. Shalom describes health, well-being, fulfillment, harmony, and an environment of joy for all.[48] Cornelius Plantinga writes:

The webbing together of God, humans, and all creation in justice, fulfillment, and delight is what the Hebrew prophets call *shalom*. We call it peace but it means far more than mere peace of mind or a cease-fire between enemies. In the Bible, shalom means *universal flourishing, wholeness and delight* – a rich state of affairs in which natural needs are satisfied and natural gifts fruitfully employed, a state of affairs that inspires joyful wonder as its Creator and Savior opens doors and welcomes the creatures in whom he delights. Shalom, in other words, is the way things ought to be.[49]

There is a reason why joy follows righteousness and peace in this Kingdom triumvirate. How could we rejoice in a world without them? Such joy would be "insulted and undone."[50] If we are living in right relationships with God and with others, peace is the harmony that results,[51] and joy is our pleasure in that concord.[52] This is healthy joy. This is the joy God seeks for us.[53] One day it will fill the earth.

When the Kingdom comes in its fullness, and the King takes his rightful place in the world, all of creation will respond in joy:

> Let the heavens be glad, and let the earth rejoice;
>> let the sea roar, and all that fills it;
>> let the field exult, and everything in it!
> Then shall all the trees of the wood sing for joy
>> before the LORD, for he comes . . . . (Psalm 96:11-12)

> Let the sea roar, and all that fills it;
>> the world and those who dwell in it!
> Let the floods clap their hands;
>> let the hills sing for joy together
>> before the LORD, for he comes . . . . (Psalm 98:7-8)

> For you shall go out in joy,
>> and be led forth in peace;

the mountains and the hills before you
   shall break forth into singing,
   and all the trees of the field shall clap their hands . . . . (Isaiah 55:12)

Should we truly imagine the whole realm of nature rejoicing in its Creator? Is this how we are to take these passages? Those of us who would feel at home in Lewis' Narnia or Tolkien's Middle Earth would love to live in such a world. At the very least these prophetic cameos tell us our joy and the joy of creation are linked, that an environment of joy is the ideal for all of creation, and that one day this will be realized.[54] (This should be the ultimate aim of our stewardship of the earth.) When the ancient harmony of Eden is restored, and raised to even greater heights in God's work of redemption, all creatures – in ways suited to their creaturehood – will reflect the glory of God, and, in that mirrored glory, will experience their share in the joy that binds all creation together with its Creator, Redeemer, and King.[55] At its fullest, our joy will be a fellowship in this cosmic joy.

Emil Brunner wrote, "A Christian is a person who not only hopes for the Kingdom of God, but one who, because he hopes for it, also does something in this world already, which he who has not this hope does not do."[56] Knowing what awaits them in the fullness of God's reign, citizens of the Kingdom give themselves to a quest for global righteousness, peace, and joy even now – with all of its implications for human relationships, their environment, and the creatures with which they share God's world.

God is not limited to our participation in his plans. He does far more apart from us than we will ever know. Nevertheless, the Kingdom is his primary answer to the problem of evil. It awaits your response and mine. Not somewhere else in a world of daydreams; here, where our actions make a difference. Not later, which becomes later, and then later; now, in this moment, and then in the next. Not through grit and determination, but in full reliance on the action of the Holy Spirit in and through us. This is the human side of how God's Kingdom will come. This is how righteousness, peace, and joy will transform our world in its great need.

QUESTIONS FOR THOUGHT AND DISCUSSION

1. Discuss this quote: "Joy is ruthlessly realistic about the world we live in, but refuses to reach the same conclusions drawn by pessimists and fatalists. Because joy is illumined by a Light they do not have, it envisions possibilities for the world that they do not see and cannot entertain." How does this compare with notions of joy that you may have had?

2. Discuss the section on Jesus and the Kingdom. How does this challenge and change your understanding of Jesus, his life, and his message?

3. Discuss this quote: "What is the Kingdom of God? As Jesus and early Christians saw it, it is the dynamic reign of God breaking into history, bringing righteousness, peace, and joy – the boon of his empire." How does this challenge or change your understanding of the Kingdom of God?

4. Discuss this quote: "The Kingdom of God is not a place, but we must still enter it. Jesus said so, and he knows better than anyone. The gateway to the Kingdom is repentance and faith." Does this get much attention in Christian circles that you know of?

5. Discuss the author's understanding of Kingdom righteousness, peace, and joy. What difference would it make if contemporary Christians understood and pursued this?

ABOUT THE AUTHOR

In 1983 Rick and Sue Howe moved to Boulder, Colorado, where they raised three children – Amberle, Lorien, and Jamison – and have devoted more than thirty years to campus ministry at the University of Colorado. In addition to writing and speaking, Rick now leads University Ministries, whose mission is to "inspire and nurture a thoughtful pursuit of Christ, one student, one professor, one university at a time." To learn more about Rick, visit his website at www.rickhowe.org. You can also follow him on Facebook at *Rick Howe on Joy* and on Twitter @rickhoweonjoy. To learn more about University Ministries, see www.university-ministries.org.

ENDNOTES

CHAPTER 1: A TALE WORTH TELLING, A STORY WORTH DEFENDING

1   St. Augustine, "Confessions," in *The Basic Writings of Saint Augustine,* ed., Whitney J. Oates (Grand Rapids: Baker Book House, 1948, repr. 1980), p. 114.

2   Aquinas, *Summa Theologica,* trans. Fathers of the English Dominican Province (London: Burns Oates & Washburn, Ltd., third ed. 1941), I, Q. 26, A. 1.

3   Per Aquinas, "God is happiness by His Essence: for He is happy not by acquisition or participation of something else, but by His Essence." Ibid., I, II, Q. 3., A. 1.

4   Karl Barth discusses the relationship between the triunity and the joy of God:

> As the triunity – and by this we mean in the strictest and most proper sense, God Himself – is the basis of the power and dignity of the divine being, and therefore, also of His self-declaration, His glory, so this triune being and life (in the strict and proper sense, God Himself) is the basis of what makes this power and dignity enlightening, persuasive and convincing. For this is the particular function of this form. *It is radiant, and what it radiates is joy. It attracts and therefore it conquers. It is, therefore, beautiful. But it is this, as we must affirm, because it reflects the triune being of God.* It does not do this materially, so that a triad is to be found in it. It does it formally, which is the only question that can now concern us. It does this to the extent that in it there is repeated and revealed the unity and distinction of the divine being particular to it as the being of the triune God. To this extent the triunity of God is the secret of His beauty. If we deny this, we at once have a God without radiance and without joy (and without humour!); a God without beauty (emphasis added).

Karl Barth, *Church Dogmatics*, eds., Geoffrey W. Bromiley, T. F. Torrance (New York: Charles Scribner's Sons, 1957), Vol. II, p. 661. Emphasis added.

5   C.S. Lewis, *Mere Christianity* (New York: Simon & Schuster. Touchstone Edition, 1996), p. 153. The quote in its context is as follows:

> Good things as well as bad, you know, are caught by a kind of infection. If you want to get warm you must stand near the fire: if you want to be wet you must get into the water. If you want joy, power, peace, eternal life, you must get close to, or even into, the thing that has them. They are not a sort of prize which God could, if He chose, just hand out to anyone. They are a great fountain of energy and beauty spurting up at the very centre of reality. If you are close to it, the spray will wet you: if you are not, you will remain dry.

6   For a development of this theme, see "The Joy of the Lord," "Joy Incarnate," and "The Joyful Spirit" in Rick Howe, *Path of Life: Finding the Joy You've Always Longed For* (Boulder, CO: University Ministries Press, Revised Edition, 2017).

7   ". . . when the morning stars sang together
      and all the sons of God shouted for joy?" (Job 38:7)

This inspired C.S. Lewis in his story of the creation of Narnia. In *The Magician's Nephew*, Lewis wrote:

> In the darkness something was happening at last. A voice had begun to sing. It was very far away and Digory found it hard to decide from what direction it was coming. Sometimes it seemed to come from all directions at once. Sometimes he almost thought it was coming out of the earth beneath them. Its lower notes were deep enough to be the voice of the earth herself. There were no words. There was hardly even a tune. But it was, beyond comparison, the most beautiful noise he had ever heard. It was so beautiful he could hardly bear it. . . .
>
> Then two wonders happened at the same moment. One was that the voice [of Aslan] was suddenly joined by other voices; more voices than you could possibly count. They were in harmony with it, but far higher up the scale: cold, tingling, silver voices. The second wonder was that the blackness overhead, all at once, was blazing with stars. They didn't come out gently one by one, as they do on a summer evening. One moment there had been nothing but darkness; next moment a thousand, thousand points of light leaped out – single stars, constellations, and planets, brighter and bigger than any in our world. There were no clouds. The new stars and the new voices began at exactly the same time. If you had seen and heard it, as Digory did, you would have felt quite certain that it was the stars themselves which were singing, and that it was the First Voice, the deep one, which had made them appear and made them sing.

C.S. Lewis, *The Magician's Nephew* (New York: NY, HarperTrophy, 1983), pp. 116-117.

8   In Anselmian terms, God is that than which no greater can be conceived. He is supreme in every conceivable way.

9   "God created the world not out of reason or necessity or practicality, but out of sheer joy. It is all gloriously superfluous." Peter Kreeft, *Heaven: The Heart's Deepest Longing* (San Francisco: Ignatius Press, 1989), p. 144.

10   Lewis Smedes, "Theology and the Playful Life," in *God and the Good: Essays in Honor of Henry Stob*, eds., Clifton Orlebeke and Lewis Smedes (Grand Rapids, MI: William B. Eerdmans Publishing Co., 1975), p. 56.

11   We see the Creator's joy in his creative work first in his benedictions over it: "And God saw that it was *good.*" (Genesis 1:10, 12, 18, 21, 25, 31)

12   A literal rendering of the name of the Garden in *The Septuagint*, the ancient Greek translation of the Hebrew Scriptures.

13   Karl Barth wrote of God and creation, "Although he did not create it divine, He did not create it ungodly, or anti-godly, but in harmony and peace with Himself, and therefore, according to His plan, as the theatre and instrument of His acts, an object of His joy and for participation in this joy. Barth, *Church Dogmatics*, Vol. 3.1, p. 102.

[14] It may be true, as Shakespeare put it, that "to err is human," but this is only true of us in our fallenness. Christians say that this was not the case with humanity-as-created-by-God.

[15] Psalm 16:4, RSV

[16] See:
> Be appalled, O heavens, at this;
>> be shocked, be utterly desolate,
>>> declares the LORD,
>> for my people have committed two evils;
>>> they have forsaken me,
>> the fountain of living waters,
>>> and hewed out cisterns for themselves,
>> broken cisterns, that can hold no water. (Jeremiah 2:10-13)

[17] "For the love of money is a root of all kinds of evils. It is through this craving that some have wandered away from the faith and pierced themselves with many pangs." (1 Timothy 6:10)

[18] See:

> I said in my heart, "Come now, I will test you with pleasure; enjoy yourself." But behold, this also was vanity. I said of laughter, "It is mad," and of pleasure, "What use is it?" I searched with my heart how to cheer my body with wine—my heart still guiding me with wisdom—and how to lay hold on folly, till I might see what was good for the children of man to do under heaven during the few days of their life. I made great works. I built houses and planted vineyards for myself. I made myself gardens and parks, and planted in them all kinds of fruit trees. I made myself pools from which to water the forest of growing trees. I bought male and female slaves, and had slaves who were born in my house. I had also great possessions of herds and flocks, more than any who had been before me in Jerusalem. I also gathered for myself silver and gold and the treasure of kings and provinces. I got singers, both men and women, and many concubines, the delight of the sons of man. So I became great and surpassed all who were before me in Jerusalem. Also my wisdom remained with me. And whatever my eyes desired I did not keep from them. I kept my heart from no pleasure, for my heart found pleasure in all my toil, and this was my reward for all my toil. (Ecclesiastes 2:1-10)

[19] Peter Kreeft, *Heaven: The Heart's Deepest Longing* (San Francisco: Ignatius Press, Expanded edition, 1980), p. 21.

[20] "But the serpent said to the woman, 'You will not surely die. For God knows that when you eat of it your eyes will be opened, and you will be like God, knowing good and evil.'" (Genesis 3:5)

[21] Ephesians 2:3

[22] The wrath of God is more than this. It includes his hatred of sin, his anger towards sin, and his judgment of sin. In Romans 1, however, wrath is God "giving sinners up" to the consequences of their sinfulness. He allows us to reject him, and to live with the

ramifications of that rejection. He steps back from us, as it were, to let our sins and their consequences play out, and in that relational distance joy is lost. That is what hell will be with unmitigated finality.

23 Kreeft, *Heaven*, p. 135.

24 ". . . while the sons of the kingdom will be thrown into the outer darkness. In that place there will be weeping and gnashing of teeth." (Matthew 8:12)

25 "You make known to me the path of life;
in your presence there is fullness of joy;
at your right hand are pleasures forevermore." (Psalm 16:11)

26 "They will suffer the punishment of eternal destruction, away from the presence of the Lord and from the glory of his might." (2 Thessalonians 1:9)

27 The sorrow of hell is unending because the sin of choosing another god is ongoing. C.S. Lewis wrote: "I willingly believe that the damned are, in one sense, successful, rebels to the end; that the doors of hell are locked on the inside." C.S. Lewis, *The Problem of Pain* (New York: Macmillan, 1962), p. 127.

28 C.S. Lewis wrote:

> There are only two kinds of people in the end: those who say to God, "Thy will be done," and those to whom God says, in the end, "Thy will be done." All that are in Hell, choose it. Without that self-choice there could be no Hell. No soul that seriously and constantly desires joy will ever miss it. Those who seek find. To those who knock it is opened.

C.S. Lewis, *The Great Divorce* (San Francisco: HarperCollins, 2001), p. 75.

29 ". . . and hope does not put us to shame, because God's love has been poured into our hearts through the Holy Spirit who has been given to us." (Romans 5:5)

30 Robert Kolb and Timothy J. Wenger eds. *The Book of Concord: The Confessions of the Evangelical Lutheran Church*, trans. Charles Arand, et al (Minneapolis: Fortress Press, 2000), p. 23.

31 Jürgen Moltmann asks this question, and finds its answer in the freedom, good will, and love of God. See Jürgen Moltmann, *Theology and Joy,* trans. Reinhard Ulrich (London: SCM Press, 1973), pp. 47ff.

32 Micah 7:18

33 Luke 12:32. "The Kingdom of God stands as a comprehensive term for all that the messianic salvation included." George Eldon Ladd, *A Theology of the New Testament* (Grand Rapids: William B. Eerdmans Publishing Co., 1974), p. 72.

34 See the following:

83

Just so, I tell you, there will be more joy in heaven over one sinner who repents than over ninety-nine righteous persons who need no repentance. (Luke 15:7, RSV)

. . . and bring the fatted calf and kill it, and let us eat and make merry; or this my son was dead, and is alive again; he was lost, and is found.' And they began to make merry. "Now his elder son was in the field; and as he came and drew near to the house, he heard music and dancing. (Luke15:23-25, RSV)

[35] Hebrews 12:2, RSV

[36] C.S. Lewis wrote, "For this tangled absurdity of a Need . . . which never fully acknowledges its own neediness, Grace substitutes a full, childlike and delighted acceptance of our Need, a joy in total dependence. We become 'jolly beggars.'" C.S. Lewis, *The Four Loves* (New York: Harcourt, Brace, Jovanovich, 1960), p. 180.

[37] See C.S. Lewis, *Mere Christianity*, p. 52.

[38] Luke 1:46-47

[39] C.S. Lewis' way of describing the Trinity. See Chapter 24, "The Three-Personal God" in his *Mere Christianity*.

[40] Josef Pieper wrote, "All love has joy as its natural fruit." Josef Pieper, *About Love* (Chicago: Franciscan Herald Press, 1974), p. 71. David Gill speaks of joy as "love's delight." See David W. Gill, *Becoming Good: Building Moral Character* (Downers Grove, Illinois: InterVarsity Press, 2000), p. 54.

[41] See:

> The earth is the LORD's and the fullness thereof;
>   the world and all who dwell in it. (Psalm 24:1)

> The heavens are yours; the earth also is yours;
>   the world and all that is in it, you have founded them. (Psalm 89:11)

[42] For instance, in the dialogue, *Phaedo*, Plato has Socrates say, "Nothing makes a thing beautiful but the presence and participation of beauty in whatever way or manner obtained . . . I stoutly contend that by beauty all beautiful things become beautiful. Plato, "Phaedo" in *Five Great Dialogues*, trans. B. Jowett, ed., Louise Ropes Loomis (New York: Walter J. Black, Inc., 1969), p. 138. See also Paul Edwards, ed., *The Encyclopedia of Philosophy* (New York: Macmillan Publishing Co., Inc., & The Free Press, 1967), Volume Six, pp. 320-324.

[43] C.S. Lewis saw them as facets of God's glory: "I was learning the far more secret doctrine that pleasures are shafts of the glory as it strikes our sensibility. As it impinges on our will or our understanding, we give it different names -- goodness or truth or the like." *C.S. Lewis, Letters to Malcolm: Chiefly on Prayer* (New York: Harcourt Brace Jovanovich, Inc., 1963), p. 89.

44   "Oh, taste and see that the LORD is good!" (Psalm 34:8)

45   We live out our days enveloped by the *sacramentum mundi* (the sacrament of the world, or the world as sacrament.)

46   John Walton sees the creation account in Genesis portraying the cosmos as a temple in which God comes to dwell, and through which he makes his glory known. John H. Walton, *The Lost World of Genesis One: Ancient Cosmology and the Origins Debate*, (Downers Grove, IL: InterVarsity Press, 2009).

The world as the theater of God's glory was a significant theme in the thought of John Calvin. See "John Calvin and the World as a Theater of God's Glory" in Belden C. Lane, *Ravished by Beauty: The Surprising Legacy of Reformed Spirituality* (Oxford: Oxford University Press, 2011), pp. 57-85.

For explorations of stewarding the earth in a Christian vision of life, see: Steven Bouma-Prediger, *For the Beauty of the Earth: A Christian Vision for Creation Care* (Grand Rapids, MI: Baker Academic, 2001); Wesley Granberg-Michaelson, ed., *Tending the Garden: Essays on the Gospel and the Earth* (Grand Rapids, MI: Eerdmans, 1987); James A. Nash, *Loving Nature: Ecological Integrity and Christian Responsibility* (Nashville: Abingdon, 1993); Francis A. Schaeffer, *Pollution and the Death of Man: The Christian View of Ecology* (Wheaton, IL: Tyndale House, 1970); Loren Wilkinson, ed., *Earthkeeping in the '90s:Stewardship of Creation* (Grand Rapids, MI: Eerdmans, 1990).

47   With future generations in mind, our responsible use of the world's resources should include renewable energy as much as possible. It is tragic not only when we, through our governments, rack up debts that will crush future generations, but when we deplete the resources of the earth, leaving future generations in peril. We should oppose both economic policies and energy policies that endanger those who come after us.

48   See:

        "Teacher, which is the great commandment in the Law?" And he said to him, "You shall love the Lord your God with all your heart and with all your soul and with all your mind. This is the great and first commandment. And a second is like it: You shall love your neighbor as yourself. On these two commandments depend all the Law and the Prophets." (Matthew 22:36-40)

49   In ancient Hebrew parlance, the word "way" is a metaphor for life, and the verb *halak*, literally to go or to walk, was used to describe the process of living. See, for instance, entry #2143 in *New International Dictionary of Old Testament Theology and Exegesis*, gen. ed., Willem A. VanGemeren (Grand Rapids, MI: Zondervan Publishing House, 1997), Vol. 1, pp. 1032-1033.

50   Jürgen Moltmann writes, "Man is to give glory to the true God and rejoice in God's and his own existence, for this by itself is meaningful enough. Joy is the meaning of human life, joy in thanksgiving and thanksgiving as joy." Moltmann, *Theology and Joy*, p. 42.

51   Augustine believed that two conditions must be met for something to be our greatest good: It must be a "good than which there is nothing better," and "it must be something which cannot be lost against the will." Augustine, "Morals,"p. 321.

52   Augustine put it this way:

> No one can be happy who does not enjoy what is man's chief good, nor is there any one who enjoys this who is not happy. (Ibid.)
> The happy life . . . (occurs) when that which is man's chief good is both loved and possessed. (Ibid.)
>
> No one is blessed who does not enjoy that which he loves. For even they who love things that ought not to be loved, do not count themselves blessed by loving merely, but by enjoying them. Who, then . . . will deny that he is blessed, who enjoys that which he loves and loves the true and highest good?. . . He who loves God is blessed in the enjoyment of God. (Augustine, *City of God*, Vol. 2, p. 110.)

Similarly, Aquinas wrote, "Man's last end may be said to be either God who is the Supreme Good absolutely; or the enjoyment of God, which denotes a certain pleasure in the last end." (Aquinas, *Summa*, I, II, Q. 3. A. 4.)

53   There are two dimensions of our chief end – glorifying God and enjoying him. We do not have two chief ends, but one with two facets (As John Piper observes in his work, *Desiring God: Meditations of a Christian Hedonist* [Portland, Oregon: Multnomah Press, 1986], p. 13. As C.S. Lewis saw it, "Fully to enjoy is to glorify. In commanding us to glorify Him, God is inviting us to enjoy Him." C.S. Lewis, *Reflections on the Psalms* [New York: Harcourt Brace Jovanovich, 1958], p. 97.)

54   Bernard Ramm calls glory "both a modality of the self-revelation of God, and an attribute of God." Bernard Ramm, *Them He Glorified* (Grand Rapids, MI: William B. Eerdmans Publishing Co., 1963), p. 10. Karl Barth wrote: "[God's glory] is God Himself in the truth and capacity and act in which He makes himself known as God." Barth, *Church Dogmatics*, Vol. II, p. 64.

55   "Lift up your heads, O gates!
>   and be lifted up, O ancient doors!
>   that the King of glory may come in." (Psalm 24:7)

56   "And Stephen said, 'Brethren and fathers, hear me. The God of glory appeared to our father Abraham.'" (Acts 7:2)

57   ". . . that the God of our Lord Jesus Christ, the Father of glory, may give you a spirit of wisdom and of revelation in the knowledge of him." (Ephesians 1:17)

58   "For when he received honor and glory from God the Father and the voice was borne to him by the Majestic Glory, "This is my beloved Son, with whom I am well pleased," (2 Peter 1:17)

59   As Jesus put it:

You are the light of the world. A city set on a hill cannot be hidden. Nor do people light a lamp and put it under a basket, but on a stand, and it gives light to all in the house. In the same way, let your light shine before others, so that they may see your good works and give glory to your Father who is in heaven. (Matthew 5:14-16)

CHAPTER 2: LAY OF THE LAND & FIRST DEFENSE: DIVINE OMNIPOTENCE

[1] Rem Edwards has written:

> It is sometimes maintained that unless a very strict proof or set of related proofs is offered, nothing is proved at all. For example, it is sometimes held that unless all the premises of an argument are absolutely certain and the pattern of reasoning indubitably valid, the proof is utterly worthless. If one adheres strictly to this rigid deductive ideal, however, one is forced to conclude that there are *no* worthwhile proofs anywhere . . . . Certainly there are no such proofs to be found in natural science or in philosophy.

Rem B. Edwards, *Reason and Religion: An Introduction to the Philosophy of Religion* (New York, NY: Harcourt, Brace and Jovanovich, 1972), p. 222.

[2] To quote Edwards again:

> Often the theistic proofs are criticized on the grounds that one is not required to accept the conclusion unless one first accepts the premises. This is true, but the theistic proofs are not peculiar in this respect. All arguments for everything everywhere are like this. If this is a weakness, it is a weakness of the entire enterprise of rationality and not simply a weakness of the philosophy of religion.

Ibid., pp. 222-223.

My claim is not that the existence of God is logically entailed in a set of assertions, but that the existence of God, compared to rival explanations, best illumines and explains our experience in the world. It is known as an argument to the best explanation. It is the kind of reasoning we routinely (and rationally) use when factual claims are involved. A jury concludes that Mr. Jones committed an armed robbery from the evidence of motive, weapon, opportunity, and an eyewitness. You conclude that it has rained from the evidence of clouds in the sky, lightening and thunder in the area, wet surfaces wherever you look, and water racing downhill on the streets of your neighborhood. Other explanations may be possible, but one is more likely than the others.

My argument is not an inference from premises that are beyond dispute, but a conclusion reached by comparing rival explanations and a range of data, including what is often called "religious experience." When the field of data is expanded to the full range of human experience and interaction with the world, and rival explanations are compared, a strong, cumulative case for the existence of God emerges. It does not prove that God exists; it strengthens the belief-worthiness of the assertion that he does. There is much that is subjective on our part, and even more that is mysterious on God's; nevertheless, the path of evidence takes us as far as reason can go, and then points beyond to forest-clad mountains and snow-capped peaks where we will find the treasure for which our hearts long.

For an introduction to this kind of argument, see, for example:

> J.P. Moreland, *Scaling the Secular City: A Defense of Christianity* (Grand Rapids, MI: Baker Book House, 1987)

> Richard Swinburne, *The Existence of God*, Second Edition (Oxford: Oxford University Press, 2004.)

> William Lane Craig, *Reasonable Faith: Christian Truth and Apologetics,* Third Edition (Wheaton, IL: Crossway Books, 2008)

> Keith Ward, *The Evidence for God: The Case for the Existence of a Spiritual Dimension*, (London: Darton, Longman & Todd, 2014).

3   "Righteous are you, O LORD, when I complain to you; yet I would plead my case before you. Why does the way of the wicked prosper? Why do all who are treacherous thrive?" (Jeremiah 12:1)

4   This is the haunting question behind the book of Job, echoed many times in the Scriptures.

5   I wrote in another volume:

> Sometimes joy banishes sorrow:

>> They shall obtain joy and gladness,
>> and sorrow and sighing shall flee away. (Isaiah 35:10)

>> Weeping may tarry for the night,
>>   but joy comes with the morning. (Psalm 30:5)

>> May those who sow in tears
>>   reap with shouts of joy!
>> He that goes forth weeping,
>>   bearing the seed for sowing,
>>   shall come home with shouts of joy. (Psalm 126:5-6)

>> You will be sorrowful, but your sorrow will turn into joy. (John 16:20)

> Other times sorrow remains, but becomes a bittersweet experience when it is touched by joy:

>> When the cares of my heart are many, your consolations cheer my soul. (Psalm 94:19)

>> Happy are those who mourn: they shall be comforted. (Matthew 5:4, JB)

We are treated as impostors, and yet are true; as unknown, and yet well known; as dying, and behold we live; as punished, and yet not killed; as sorrowful, yet always rejoicing. (2 Corinthians 6:9-10)

It is not that sorrow and joy come one after the other; they are facets of the same experience. I have known this myself (as you may have) when, in grieving over the death of a loved one, joy comes quietly and gently, not removing sorrow, but transposing the lament into a calm and soothing key. Joy in the midst of sorrow is like a soft light illumining the darkness, or the pleasure of a crying child in the comfort of her mother's loving arms.

See Rick Howe, *Path of Life: Finding the Joy You've Always Longed For* (Boulder, CO: University Ministries Press, Revised Edition, 2017), pp. 27-28.

6   In the history of religion, there have been traditions that see good and evil as equal, opposite, cosmic forces or deities. Dualistic thought had is origins in the ancient Persian and Middle-Eastern worlds, found in Zoroastrianism and later in Manichaeism.

7   See Genesis 1:10, 12, 18, 21, 25, 31, where God pronounces his creation good, and very good.

Depending upon the translation, there are two verses in the Old Testament that seem to say that God does, in fact create evil. The first is Isaiah 45:7. In the King James Version it reads: "I form the light, and create darkness: I make peace, and create evil: I the LORD do all these things." The second is Amos 3:6, which, in the King James Version reads, "Shall a trumpet be blown in the city, and the people not be afraid? Shall there be evil in a city, and the LORD hath not done it?"

In Hebrew, the word translated "evil" in these verses is *rah*. The field of meaning for this word includes moral evil. In the King James Version, however, it is also translated hurt, harm, ill, sorrow, mischief, displeased, adversity, affliction, trouble, calamity, grievous, misery, and trouble. These are all possible translations – even for that version. *Rah* can mean something that is not good for us, in the sense that it causes pain. For instance, it is used in Jeremiah 24:2 of "bad" figs. If you eat them, you may get sick! It is also used in Proverbs 15:10 of correction, or discipline. It is evil in the sense that it might involve pain.

Modern translations translate *rah* in Isaiah 45:7 as "calamity," and in Amos 3:6 as "calamity" or "disaster." This is what we would call "natural evil" in our discussion. God does take responsibility for this, but it is not the same as "moral evil."

8   Christians regard Satan as chief among the "fallen angels" – angelic beings who were created good, but who fell in a primordial rebellion against God.

9   C.S. Lewis, *Mere Christianity* (New York: Macmillan Publishing Co., 1952), p. 45.

10   Rick Howe, *River of Delights: Quenching Your Thirst For Joy*, Volume 2 (Boulder, CO: University Ministries Press, Revised Edition, 2017), p. 150.

[11] In the prologue of Job, Satan is responsible for human sickness and death, and the death of animals. He is a causal agent behind "fire from heaven" a deadly "great wind," and human violence in the story. In the Gospels demonic beings are forces behind human sickness and infirmity, and the death of animals. For a treatment of the significance of demonic evil in the larger context of the problem of evil, see Gregory Boyd, *Satan and the Problem of Evil* (Downers Grove, IL: IVP Academic, 2001).

[12] C.S. Lewis wrote "There are two equal and opposite errors into which our race can fall about the devils. One is to disbelieve in their existence. The other is to believe, and to feel an excessive and unhealthy interest in them. They themselves are equally pleased by both errors, and hail a materialist or magician with the same delight" C.S. Lewis. *The Screwtape Letters* (New York: HarperCollins, 1996) p. ix.

[13] See, for instance, Genesis 3 and Romans 5:12-21.

[14] "And the Lord God commanded the man, saying, 'You may surely eat of every tree of the garden, but of the tree of the knowledge of good and evil you shall not eat, for in the day that you eat of it you shall surely die." (Genesis 2:16-17) See also Genesis 3:1ff.

[15] The fallen condition of the world is not merely a result of human freedom. It is also God's judgment on human sin. We must not only come to grips with the divine blessing upon our world (Genesis 1), but a divine curse because of our sin (Genesis 3). Together, they provide a general background for our experience in the world pleasure on the one hand, and pain and suffering on the other – the first an expression of God's goodness toward sinners, and the second, an expression of his judgment upon their sin. Some (but not all) instances of pain and suffering are judicially related to God. There are times in the Scriptures when God does bring pain and suffering to people as punishment for sin. But not all pain and suffering can be explained this way (as in the famous case of Job). As the state punishes wrongdoers, with the result that their pain and suffering is just, so God magnifies his justice through the punishment of sin, whether it is served indirectly through moral agents or natural forces, or directly by him. The greater good served in such instances is the glory of God. If God does not exercise justice, or frees sinners from the just consequences of their sin, it is God exercising mercy.

[16] I take "total depravity" to mean not that we are as bad as we can be, but that sinfulness taints every facet of our humanity.

[17] Dallas Willard wrote: "Full joy is our first line of defense against weakness, failure, and disease of mind and body." Dallas Willard, *Renovation of the Heart: Putting on the Character of Christ* (Colorado Springs, CO: NavPress, 2002), p. 133.

Peter Kreeft makes the same point: "A joyful spirit inspires joyful feelings and even a more psychosomatically healthy body. (For example, we need less sleep when we have joy and have more resistance to all kinds of diseases from colds to cancers.)" Peter Kreeft, *Heaven: The Heart's Deepest Longing* (San Francisco: Ignatius Press, Expanded Edition, 1980), p. 129.

¹⁸ This is the joy which Madeleine L'Engle sees captured in the Sanskrit word *ananda*: "that joy in existence, without which the universe will fall apart and collapse." Madeleine L'Engle, *A Swiftly Tilting Planet* (New York, NY: Dell Publishing, 1979), p. 40. It is the joy that binds Being to being, and all created things to each other. It is the aim of creation and redemption alike.

¹⁹ In the Garden story, God's curse upon human sin was multi-faceted, and included the relationship between humans and their natural environment. The apostle Paul commented:

> For the creation was subjected to futility, not willingly, but because of him who subjected it, in hope that the creation itself will be set free from its bondage to corruption and obtain the freedom of the glory of the children of God. For we know that the whole creation has been groaning together in the pains of childbirth until now. (Romans 8:20-22)

This will be remedied in what the New Testament calls the Resurrection, or the New Heavens and New Earth:

> For behold, I create new heavens and a new earth, and the former things shall not be remembered or come into mind. (Isaiah 65:17)

> But according to his promise we are waiting for new heavens and a new earth in which righteousness dwells. (2 Peter 3:13)

> Then I saw a new heaven and a new earth, for the first heaven and the first earth had passed away, and the sea was no more. (Revelation 21:2)

²⁰ In other words, it is not only what we do individually and as a race that impacts the world. Who we are and who we are becoming, individually and as a race, have repercussions for the health and well-being of our planet.

²¹ Whether it involves human negligence or malevolence, many of the evils that we might consider *natural* turn out to be directly or indirectly the result of *moral* evil.

The contemporary issue of global warming helps us understand how humans can use their moral freedom in ways that impact our planet, and even produce phenomena, such as flooding and drought, that earlier generations would have seen as natural evil. They are regarded as *anthropogenic*, that is, they are brought about, directly or indirectly, by the activity of humans.

²² C.S. Lewis, *The Problem of Pain* (New York, NY: HarperOne, 2001). P. 31.

²³ See Psalm 16:11 –

> You make known to me the path of life;
>   in your presence there is fullness of joy;
>   at your right hand are pleasures forevermore.

24   If you think of joy as a private, personal experience that is unrelated to life, you will miss its significance for the problem of evil. For an in-depth exploration of joy as an integrating motif in all of life, see Rick Howe, *Path of Life: Finding the Joy You've Always Longed For* (Boulder, CO: University Ministries Press, Revised Edition, 2017), and Rick Howe, *Rivers of Delight: Quenching Your Thirst for Joy, Volumes 1 and 2* (Boulder, CO: University Ministries Press, Revised Editions, 2017).

25   In my understanding of freedom, we are free if, given the identical antecedents leading to a decision, we could have chosen otherwise. I would add quickly, however, that though we *could* have done otherwise, in most instances we *would* not have. We only think we would have with the benefit of hindsight. But the addition of a retrospective look at the situation and the events that emerged from it means that the set of antecedents which led to the original decision is no longer intact. The antecedents would no longer be identical. Remove all post-decision factors, replay the exact set of antecedents again, and, even though we could have chosen otherwise, we rarely (if ever?) would.

That we *could* have done otherwise is a metaphysical issue; whether we *would* have done otherwise is a moral issue. Facing a similar situation, and choosing to respond differently (especially after processing and evaluating our earlier decision and everything that followed from it), is what it means to grow in wisdom. That is another issue.

While this understanding of freedom best fits the moral reasoning of the Scriptures, it does not mean that we can do anything we want. We are significantly free, but not absolutely free. Ours is a boundaried freedom, with limits determined by God.

The book of Job provides us with this notion of boundaries set by God. Of his work in the realm of nature, God says:

> Or who shut in the sea with doors, when it burst forth from the womb; when I made clouds its garment, and thick darkness its swaddling band, and prescribed bounds for it, and set bars and doors, and said, 'Thus far shall you come, and no farther, and here shall your proud waves be stayed'? (38:10-11, RSV. See also Psalm 104:5-9)

The first two chapters of the book of Job show God operating in the same way with moral agents. God gives Satan (a supernatural moral agent, but a moral agent nonetheless) freedom to act, but sets the boundaries of his freedom at the same time (1:12; 2:6).

The apostle Paul saw this same pattern to God's relation to human nations: "And he made from one every nation of men to live on all the face of the earth, having determined allotted periods and the boundaries of their habitation" (Acts 17:26, RSV).

When Paul tells believers that God will not allow them to be tested beyond their strength (1 Corinthians 10:13), he is assuring them that God in his sovereign wisdom and loving commitment to them knows where to fix the boundaries in their lives (which includes, in many cases, setting the boundaries of what he will allow other free agents to do to them).

The freedom that God gives always takes place within the boundaries that he has established. They are boundaries of time and place, nature and nurture, and God's own providential acts in the course of life – all of which provide room for a significant degree of freedom, but at the same time protect, preserve and fulfill his sovereign plan.

Although I am wary of some of the ways in which this analogy can be used, there is some merit in seeing similarities between divine providence and a game of chess. God is the Chess Master, and we are on the other side of the board. We have freedom to move our pieces, but it is not absolute. There are limiting factors: the board itself, the chess pieces, the rules of the game, moves that have already been made, moves that will be made by the Master, and our own limitations in the decision-making dynamics of the game. Our freedom has boundaries.

[26] In the inimitable words of C.S. Lewis:

> God created things which had free will. That means creatures which can go either wrong or right. Some people think they can imagine a creature which was free but had no possibility of going wrong; I cannot. If a thing is free to be good it is also free to be bad. And free will is what has made evil possible. Why, then, did God give them free will? Because free will, though it makes evil possible, is also the only thing that makes possible any love or goodness or joy worth having. A world of automata – of creatures that worked like machines – would hardly be worth creating. *The happiness which God designs for His higher creatures is the happiness of being freely, voluntarily united to Him and to each other in an ecstasy of love and delight compared with which the most rapturous love between a man and a woman on this earth is mere milk and water. And for that they must be free.*

C.S. Lewis, *Mere Christianity*, p. 52. Emphasis added.

Peter Van Inwagen writes:

> Human beings have not been made merely to mouth words of praise or to be passively awash in a pleasant sensation of the presence of God. They have been made to be intimately aware of God and capable of freely acting on this awareness; having seen God, they may either glorify and enjoy what they have seen – the glorification and the enjoyment are separate only by the intellect in an act of severe abstraction – or they may reject what they have seen and attempt to order their own lives and to create their own objects of enjoyment. The choice is theirs and it is a free choice: to choose either way is genuinely open to each human being.

> God wishes to be the object of human glorification and enjoyment not out of vanity, but out of love: He is glorious and enjoyable to a degree infinitely greater than that of any other object. He has given us free will in this matter because it is only when a person, having contemplated the properties of something, freely assents to the proposition that that thing is worthy of glory, and then proceeds freely to offer glory to it, that a thing is truly glorified. And it is only when a person, having enjoyed a thing, freely chooses to continue in the enjoyment of that thing that true enjoyment occurs.

Peter Van Inwagen, "Non Est Hick" in *The Rationality of Belief & the Plurality of Faith,* Thomas D. Senor, ed., (Ithaca and London: Cornell University Press, 1995), pp. 220-221.

[27]   See the following:

> God is not man, that he should lie,
>   or a son of man, that he should change his mind.
> Has he said, and will he not do it?
>   Or has he spoken, and will he not fulfill it? (Numbers 23:19)

> . . . in hope of eternal life, which God, who never lies, promised before the ages began. (Titus 1:2)

> . . . so that by two unchangeable things, in which it is impossible for God to lie, we who have fled for refuge might have strong encouragement to hold fast to the hope set before us. (Hebrews 6:18)

[28]   See the following:

> "O my God," I say, "take me not away
>   in the midst of my days—
>   you whose years endure
>   throughout all generations!"
>   Of old you laid the foundation of the earth,
>   and the heavens are the work of your hands.
>   They will perish, but you will remain;
>   they will all wear out like a garment.
>   You will change them like a robe, and they will pass away,
>   but you are the same, and your years have no end. (Psalm 102:24-27)

> "For I the Lord do not change; therefore you, O children of Jacob, are not consumed." (Malachi 3:6)

> Every good gift and every perfect gift is from above, coming down from the Father of lights with whom there is no variation or shadow due to change. (James 1:17)

[29]   See 2 Timothy 2:13 -

> If we are faithless, he remains faithful—
> for he cannot deny himself.

[30]   See St. Thomas Aquinas, *Summa Theologica* trans., Fathers of the English Dominican Province, (U.S.A.: Benzinger Brothers 1947), I, I, Q. 25, A. 3.

[31]   This is what it means to say that God is a necessary being.

[32]   Theologians use the word *aseity* for this, which means that God exists in and of himself. He is not dependent upon anything outside himself for his existence.

[33]   If God is the Supreme Being, that is, he is that than which no greater can be conceived (Anselm), it is logically impossible for him to be more or less than he is.

[34]   The Nicene Creed, as given in the First Council of Constantinople (381) speaks of the Son as "begotten from the Father before all time, Light from Light, true God from true God, begotten not created" and of the Spirit as "the Lord and life-giver, Who proceeds

from the Father, Who is worshiped and glorified together with the Father and the Son." See John H. Leith, ed., *Creeds of the Churches: A Reader in Christian Doctrine from the Bible to the Present*, third edition, (Louisville: John Knox Press, 1982), p. 33

[35] Some critics contend that these concessions defeat the claim that God is omnipotent. I disagree. If it comes down to it, however, Christians can frame the power of God in terms of supreme power, or being "almighty," and lose nothing that is essential to the faith. See Chapter 4 of Thomas V. Morris, *Our Idea of God: An Introduction to Philosophical Theology* (Downers Grove, IL: InterVarsity Press, 1991) for other ways of thinking about the power of God.

[36] C.S. Lewis, *The Problem of Pain*, p. 18.

[37] Earlier in this chapter I spoke of evil in the natural world that has come about from the Fall of our first parents into sin. Whether one views this as God's punishment upon sin, or a world that has gone awry because of sin, it is possible that many (some would say all) natural evils have their source in moral evil. While it may have seemed far-fetched at one time, it is now commonly accepted in scientific circles that many natural phenomena, such as the melting of glaciers, flooding and drought, and even hurricanes, may be *anthropogenic*, that is brought about by human factors at play in the environment.

Earlier in this chapter I also wrote about demonic evil. Although they may not be able to identify or quantify it, Christians who accept the reality of the demonic nevertheless say that we must also take moral evil on a higher plane into account in the disruption of natural forces at play in the world.

[38] J.L. Mackie wrote:

> If God has made men such that in their free choices they sometimes prefer what is good and sometimes what is evil, why could he not have made men such that they always freely choose the good? If there is no logical impossibility in a man's choosing the good on one, or on several occasions, there cannot be a logical impossibility in his freely choosing the good on every occasion. God was not, then, faced with a choice between making innocent automata and making beings who, in acting freely, would sometimes go wrong: there was open to him the obviously better possibility of making beings who would act freely but always go right. Clearly, his failure to avail himself of this possibility is inconsistent with his being both omnipotent and wholly good.

See J.L. Mackie, "Evil and Omnipotence" in William L. Rowe, ed., *God and the Problem of Evil* (Malden, MA: Blackwell Publishers, 2001), p. 86.

[39] It may seem that the eternal state of the redeemed will be just such a world, inhabited by morally free creatures who always choose good. The inhabitants of the new heavens and earth will not be *de novo* creations, however, but resurrected and redeemed sinners. To our point, they will be morally free agents who have chosen evil. That world will come into being through a total transformation of morally free creatures who were once moral failures. Redemption is predicated upon Creation and the Fall, and brings about possibilities that would not otherwise come about.

40   It is possible that all possible free creatures suffer from what Plantinga calls "transworld depravity." "What is important about the idea of transworld depravity," Plantinga claims, "is that if a person suffers from it, then it wasn't within God's power to actualize any world in which that person is significantly free but does no wrong – that is, a world in which he produces moral good but no moral evil." See Alvin Plantinga, *God, Freedom, and Evil* (Grand Rapids, MI: Eerdmans, 1977), p. 48.

41   If there were a way to assess logical possibilities beyond the bare fact that they are logically possible, our experience of moral agents is uniform and without exception: We have experience of moral agents who choose evil, and no experience whatsoever of moral agents who always choose good and never evil.

42   Christians can avoid the problems that beset the best-of-all-possible-worlds by talking instead about a world that best serves the purposes of an omnipotent, supremely good God. In Christian theology, that will be the new heavens and new earth. This world is a necessary means to that world to come.

43   A number of philosophers believe that the notion of the best of all possible worlds is incoherent, including Brian Leftow, Alvin Plantinga, Richard Swinburne, Dean Zimmerman, Timothy O'Conner and Michael Almeida. See *the Closer to Truth* video series found at: https://www.closertotruth.com/series/the-best-all-possible-worlds.

CHAPTER 3: SECOND DEFENSE: DIVINE GOODNESS

1   There is enough food in the world to feed the entire world. That is God's gift. That is the expression of his goodness. The problem of starvation is one of human stewardship and the management and distribution of resources, whether on a large scale or in a small, local setting.

     What about famine and drought? They, too, can be "anthropogenic," that is, they can be brought about directly or indirectly by human factors, such as global warming and climate change. They are features of a world that is no longer in harmony with the purposes of the Creator. In the Bible, famine and drought often mirror the spiritual conditions of a people, and are used by God to disrupt a sinful status quo and bring about repentance, faith, and obedience – which, I would argue, is a potential greater good.

2   Genesis 1:26, NRSV.

3   See William L. Rowe, *Philosophy of Religion: An Introduction* (Encino, CA: Dickenson, 1978), p. 89.

4   Critics also cite examples of animal pain as gratuitous evil. The problem of animal pain is important, but would take me too far from my focus on joy and the problem of evil. To explore this issue further, see Chapter IX, "Animal Pain" in C.S. Lewis, *The Problem of Pain* (New York: Macmillan, 1962). For a more recent treatment, see Michael J. Murray, *Nature Red in Tooth and Claw: Theism and the Problem of Animal Suffering*

(Oxford University Press, 2009).

5   "Rejoice with those who rejoice, weep with those who weep." (Romans 12:15)

6   Forthcoming, 2017. See Chapter 2, "On Second Thought."

7   The more sympathetic, compassionate, or concerned about justice we are, the more powerfully these emotions shape our beliefs. This doesn't mean that if we are sympathetic, compassionate, or concerned about justice, we will deny the existence of God because there is evil in the world. Jesus was all of these things, but did not. When he was told by Mary of the death of his friend, Lazarus, the Gospel of John says: "When Jesus saw her weeping . . . he was deeply moved in his spirit and greatly troubled. . . . Jesus wept." (John 11:33-35) These are emotions of sorrow and indignation in the face of evil. If you grant the high Christology of the Gospel of John, this is God himself railing against evil in his world. For many, these strong emotions animate and shape a belief in God that finds its practical expression in acts of kindness and mercy, and the pursuit of justice.

8   Which is to say that the success of the evidential problem of evil depends largely upon the emotional or existential problem of evil.

9   By the nature of the case, if an evil has been prevented, we will not be able to see it because it did not happen. Sometimes, however, looking back on a situation we have a sense of "what might have been" if other circumstances had played out, and we see how a greater evil did not happen that might have.

10 William Rowe makes this distinction in his case for "friendly atheism," the view that an atheist can acknowledge that theists are rational in their belief that God exists, even if it is the case that he does not. In my view, Christians should extend this same "principle of charity" to atheists, even when we have strong disagreements about what is true. See "The Problem of Evil and Some Varieties of Atheism" in *The Evidential Argument from Evil*, Daniel Howard-Snyder, ed. (Bloomington, IN: Indiana University Press, 1996).

In my work, *Reasons of the Heart: Joy and the Rationality of Faith*, I write:

> Rationality and truth belong together, but are not bound together. It is possible to be rational in believing something that is false, and possible to come to a true belief irrationally. Let me illustrate. Suppose, after listening to days of evidence and arguments, that a jury reached the verdict that Mr. Smith killed his wife. Given the case that was presented to them, and their open and honest evaluation, let's grant that it was the rational thing to do. That belief could be false. We have all heard of guilty verdicts that were later overturned when new evidence surfaced that vindicated the defendant. Suppose that Mr. Smith had an identical twin brother who actually committed the heinous crime and fled the country, leaving his look-alike brother to take the rap. You would have people who are rational in a belief (given the evidence presented in

court and their open-minded and careful evaluation) that is false (because Mr. Smith didn't do it).

Suppose, however, that one member of the jury secretly believed that Mr. Smith was innocent. If, in fact, Mr. Smith's twin brother set him up to take the blame for the murder, that juror would have a true belief. But let's say that he did not reach his conclusion by considering the evidence and arguments presented in court. Imagine instead that he violated the court's order not to discuss the trial with anyone, and that he told his wife, who in turn consulted a medium, who, in a séance, purportedly asked the dead woman if she had been killed by her husband, and was purportedly told that someone else had done the dastardly deed. Most of us would agree that this juror's belief in Mr. Smith's innocence is true (because Mr. Smith didn't commit the crime) but irrational (because it was not formed in a rational manner).

Rick Howe, *Reasons of the Heart: Joy and the Rationality of Faith* (Boulder, CO: University Ministries Press, 2017), pp. 44-45.

[11] Some of these theological considerations are not implied by the existence of a good, all-powerful God. Nevertheless, they are compatible with the existence of such a God, and are part of the rich, Christian theological tradition associated with belief in such a God.

[12] C.S. Lewis believed that God brings a complex good from a simple evil:

> In the fallen and partially redeemed universe we may distinguish (1) the simple good descending from God, (2) the simple evil produced by rebellious creatures, and (3) the exploitation of that evil by God for His redemptive purpose, which produces (4) the complex good to which accepted suffering and repented sin contribute.

C.S. Lewis, *The Problem of Pain*, p. 111.

This is illustrated by J.R.R. Tolkien's notion of *eucatastrophe*, or a "good catastrophe." He used this as a literary motif in his stories:

> The eucatastrophic tale is the true form of fairy-tale, and its highest function . . . . It does not deny the existence of *dyscatastrophe*, of sorrow and failure: the possibility of these is necessary to the joy of deliverance; it denies . . . universal final defeat and in so far is *evangelium*, giving a fleeting glimpse of Joy, Joy beyond the walls of the world, poignant as grief . . . . In such stories . . . we get a piercing glimpse of joy, and heart's desire, that for a moment passes outside the frame, rends indeed the very web of story, and lets a gleam come through.

J.R.R. Tolkien, *The Tolkien Reader* (New York: Ballentine Books, 1966), pp. 86-87.

There are *dyscatastrophes* in our world. Sorrow, suffering, and evil are painful realities, but not the final reality. They are darkness in our world. Eucatastrophe is a shaft of light piercing that darkness. It is God bringing a small good from sorrow and failure –

often in unexpected and even surprising ways – as a preview of the far greater good that he will bring at the end of time. Until deliverance comes, evil seems gratuitous.

13 Or a greater evil may not be prevented similarly because its prevention depended on acts of morally free agents that do not occur.

14 Which is to say that an evil may be gratuitous in the narrow sense that a specific greater good does not result from it, but not gratuitous in a broader sense, because it serves the greater good of a world in which free moral agents can choose good or evil.

Alvin Plantinga has written:

> God's creation of persons with morally significant free will is something of tremendous value. God could not eliminate much of the evil and suffering in this world without thereby eliminating the greater good of having created persons with free will with whom he could have relationships and who are able to love one another and do good deeds.

Quoted in the *Internet Encyclopedia of Philosophy*, "The Logical Problem of Evil," by James R. Beebe, found at: http://www.iep.utm.edu/evil-log/#H4.

15 In the case of our imagined theft, I would say further that God knew beforehand that these moral agents would not act to bring about these greater goods, and that he factored this into a larger plan in which, nevertheless, the theft of $100 ultimately brings about a greater good or prevents a greater evil that is known to him, if not yet to Ms. Smith. Although evil entered the world through Fred Wilson's theft, the will of a good, all-powerful God will prevail. Even if it is not the good that God prepared if we had obeyed him, as Ransom says in C.S. Lewis's *Perelandra*, "Whatever you do, He will make good of it." C.S. Lewis, *Perelandra* (New York, NY: Scribner, 1996), p. 96.

16 Calvinists traditionally affirm that God knows the future, but deny the kind of moral freedom that I have posited for human beings. An emerging group of Christian philosophers and theologians advocate what is known as "open theism," a view in which libertarian freedom is affirmed, but God's knowledge of the future, insofar as it is contingent on the actions of morally free agents, is denied or highly qualified. I hold a middle position that affirms libertarian freedom and an understanding of the omniscience of God that includes the future actions of moral agents who possess libertarian freedom. For a survey of views on these issues, see *Divine Foreknowledge: Four Views*, edited by James K. Beilby and Paul R. Eddy (Downers Grove, IL: InterVarsity Press, 2001). See also http://www.reasonablefaith.org/scholarly-articles/divine-omniscience for articles by William Lane Craig on divine omniscience and human freedom.

17 Further back, believers say that the very notion of moral evil – even on the lips of atheists – implies the existence of God.

If Christianity is true, our ability to evaluate life in moral categories such as right and wrong, good and evil, just and unjust, is a finite reflection of the moral agency of God.

(To say that God is a moral agent is to say that he possesses and exercises powers of moral agency, such as intelligence and volition, and possesses dispositions to act in certain ways and not in others, which he characterizes as good and evil.) If, for the sake of argument, there is no such God, and that we do not bear his image, how is it that we have come to regard some things in the world as "evil?"

This wouldn't be a problem if the word "evil" were just a code word for something that we don't happen to like, or something that frustrates our desires and aspirations. While some people might think that way, there are many who go beyond that in their understanding of evil. Whether they are right or wrong, they regard evil as something that is inherently out of harmony with the "way things should be."

C.S. Lewis put it this way: "My argument against God was that the universe seemed so cruel and unjust. But how had I got this idea of just and unjust? A man does not call a line crooked unless he has some idea of a straight line. What was I comparing this universe with when I called it unjust?" C.S. Lewis, *Mere Christianity*, Simon and Schuster, Touchstone Edition, 1996), p. 45.

If God doesn't exist, how is it that there are creatures in this world who are able to form the moral judgment that there is evil in the world? It is a fact that demands an explanation, and one that fits. This is known as a *moral argument for the existence of God*. For more on this, see the following:

> William Lane Craig, "Five Reasons Why God Exists" in *God: A Debate Between a Christian and an Atheist*, ed., William Lane Craig and Walter Sinnott-Armstrong (New York: Oxford University Press, 2004).

> C. Stephen Evans, "Moral Arguments for the Existence of God," in the Stanford Encyclopedia of Philosophy, found at http://plato.stanford.edu/entries/moral-arguments-god/.

[18]   Stephen Wykstra, calls this a "Noseeum Move," that is, "We no see 'um, so they don't exist." See "Rowe's Noseeum Arguments from Evil" in Howard-Snyder, *Evidential Argument*.

[19]   Believers fare no better. Even if we say that we know something of God's purposes, broadly speaking, we are not in a position to know what specific greater good might come, or what specific greater evil might be averted, if God permits an evil to occur. This situation arises inevitably from the epistemic distance between God and mortals. An omniscient God knows things that we do not. See William P. Alston, "The Inductive Argument from Evil and the Human Cognitive Condition," in Howard-Snyder, *Evidential Argument*, ibid, and Paul Draper, "The Skeptical Theist," ibid.

[20]   If there were a solution, someone with greater knowledge and skills would be able to see it.

[21]   This is an example of what is known as a "G.E. Moore shift," standing an opponent's argument on its head by denying the conclusion of the argument and making the denial a premise in one's own. For more on this, see William L. Rowe, "The Problem of Evil and Some Varieties of Atheism" in Howard-Snyder, *Evidential Argument*. Ibid.

[22] See my forthcoming work, *Reasons of the Heart: Joy and the Rationality of Faith*, 2017 for reasons for believing that God exists. There are many others. A short list of helpful sources by date includes:

Does God Exist?: The Debate Between Theists & Atheists, J. P. Moreland and Kai Nielsen Prometheus Books, 1993

GOD?: A Debate Between a Christian and an Atheist, William Lane Craig and Walter Sinnott-Armstrong, Oxford University Press, 2004

Richard Swinburne, *Is There a God?* Revised Edition, Oxford University Press, 2010

C. Stephen Evans *Why Christian Faith Still Makes Sense: A Response to Contemporary Challenges* Baker Academic, 2015

[23] I haven't taken the time or space to address the issue of horrendous evil. The problem of evil is at its most challenging when it seems horrendous to us, whether this has to do with magnitude, intensity, or both. Horrendous evil, critics say, can involve moral evil or natural evil. Horrendous evil has a gratuitous element. Its victims do not appear to be positioned for a greater good or to escape a greater evil.

Marilyn McCord Adams gives the following examples of horrendous moral evil:

> I offer the following list of paradigmatic horror: the rape of a woman and axing off of her arms, psycho-physical torture whose ultimate goal is the disintegration of personality, betrayal of one's deepest loyalties, child abuse of the sort described by Ivan Karamazov, child pornography, parental incest, slow death by starvation, the explosion of nuclear bombs over populated areas, having to choose which one of one's children shall live and which will be executed by terrorists, being the accidental and/or unwitting agent of the disfigurement or death of those one loves best. I regard these as paradigmatic, because I believe most people would find in the doing or suffering of them prima-facie reason to doubt the positive meaning of their lives.

"Horrendous Evils and the Goodness of God," *The Problem of Evil* (ed., Marilyn McCord Adams and Robert Merrihew Adams (New York: Oxford University Press, 1990, pp. 211-12.

Apart from their gut-wrenching emotional impact, at the end of the day believers say that such evil exists because of human freedom and depravity, and a world impacted and skewed by the evil of its inhabitants. If God bestows the kind of moral freedom that we have stipulated, then free-willed moral agents can use their will for good or evil – even if their choice involves horrendous evil. A world in which free-willed creatures can choose good or evil is better than a world without them.

[24] John R. W. Stott, *The Cross of Christ* (Downers Grove, IL: InterVarsity Press, 2006), pp. 326-327.

[25] For a robust development of this view, see Marilyn McCord Adams, *Horrendous Evils and the Goodness of God* (Ithaca, NY: Cornell University Press, 1999).

CHAPTER 4: THIS WORLD AND THE NEXT: A THEODICY

1   From the last chapter:

> I concede that gratuitous evil exists in appearance and in a contingent relationship with human freedom. I deny the existence of evil that is categorically gratuitous. If this sort of evil existed, it would be evil whose gratuitous character is simple, unqualified, and absolute. It would be evil that serves no greater good or prevents no greater evil in any logically possible world in which it exists.

To repeat my argument from the last chapter:

(1)   If a good, all-powerful God exists, absolute gratuitous evil does not exist.
(2)   A good, all-powerful God exists;
(3)   Therefore, absolute gratuitous evil does not exist.

2   In the last chapter I conceded that gratuitous evil exists in a contingent relationship with human freedom. God cannot remove the possibility of such evil without removing the freedom that makes it possible. But this is to say that such evil is not gratuitous after all, since it serves the greater good of a world in which there are free moral agents who can choose good or evil.

3   Literally, a justification of God. The term was coined by the 18th century philosopher and mathematician, Gottfried Wilhelm Leibniz. See his *Theodicy*, ed., Diogenes Allen (Indianapolis, New York: The Bobbs-Merrill Company, Inc., 1966).

4   The Westminster Confession strikes a wise balance on the perspicuity of Scripture:

> All things in Scripture are not alike plain in themselves, nor alike clear unto all: yet those things which are necessary to be known, believed, and observed for salvation are so clearly propounded, and opened in some place of Scripture or other, that not only the learned, but the unlearned, in a due use of the ordinary means, may attain unto a sufficient understanding of them.

The Westminster Confession of Faith, 1.7, found at:
http://www.reformed.org/documents/wcf_with_proofs/

5   A greater good may come only on the other side of (and even through) sorrow and suffering when evil is prolonged and seems gratuitous. Depending on our response, it may grow into bitterness and resentment, or it may be redemptive. It may lead to a greater evil, or it may contain the seeds of a greater good if, in our lament, we are brought to a place of a humble surrender and openness to God. "He who goes out weeping, bearing the seed for sowing, shall come home with shouts of joy, bringing his sheaves with him." (Psalm 126:6.)

6   C.S. Lewis, *The Problem of Pain* (New York: HarperOne, 2001), p.91.

Eleanor Stump has written:

> Natural evil—the pain of disease, the intermittent and unpredictable destruction of natural disasters, the decay of old age, the imminence of death—takes away a person's satisfaction with himself. It tends to humble him, show him his frailty, make him reflect on the transience of temporal goods, and turn his affections towards other-worldly things, away from the things of this world. No amount of moral or natural evil, of course, can guarantee that a man will [place his faith in God]. . . . But evil of this sort is the best hope, I think, and maybe the only effective means, for bringing men to such a state.

See Eleanore Stump, "The Problem of Evil" in Eleanore Stump and Michael J. Murray, eds., *Philosophy of Religion: The Big Questions* (Malden, MA: Blackwell Publishers, Ltd., 1999), p. 233.

7   There comes a time when we cannot do something because we become entrenched in willing not to do it. Like an addiction, we can give in to sin until we are trapped by it. As both Jesus and Paul put it, we become slaves to sin.

> Jesus answered them, "Truly, truly, I say to you, everyone who practices sin is a slave to sin." (John 8:34)

> Do you not know that if you present yourselves to anyone as obedient slaves, you are slaves of the one whom you obey, either of sin, which leads to death, or of obedience, which leads to righteousness? But thanks be to God, that you who were once slaves of sin have become obedient from the heart to the standard of teaching to which you were committed. (Romans 6:16-17)

8   Christians believe that as the joys of heaven surpass all that we know, so the pain and suffering of hell are likely greater than anything we can imagine. If this is true, critics say, then hell is a more serious objection to the existence of a good, all-powerful God than evil in this world. See Marilyn McCord Adams, "The Problem of Hell: A Problem of Evil for Christians," in William L. Rowe, ed., *God and the Problem of Evil* (Molden, MA: Blackwell Publishers, 2001).

For my part, I don't think we know as much about hell as some people think we do. I am a reverent agnostic about much of it. We are on the surest footing, first, if we stay close to the teaching of Jesus. In an earlier chapter I wrote:

> We are all sons of Adam and daughters of Eve. We have all shared in their sin and know their consequent sorrow.

> This is the condition of fallen humanity. This is what it means to be "by nature children of wrath." The wrath of God is not a bolt of lighting, thrown Zeus-like from the heavens to punish wrongdoers. Wrath is joy rejected. Peter Kreeft is right: "But the opposite of true joy is far worse than anguish . . . . In fact, its opposite is hell." Jesus' description of perdition is no pre-scientific fiction. It is as realistic as anything can be. Hell is a place of weeping and gnashing of teeth. Ultimate sorrow and grief. If joy is found only in the undimmed presence of God, and hell is the darkness of eternal separation from him, there is no other way that it could be. Hell is the place of divine wrath: joy refused and forfeited with finality. It is the unending, unmitigated sorrow of

choosing another god. It became one of two destinies the day our first parents took their first steps from the Garden.

We are on sure footing, too, if we follow the trajectory of other beliefs that we have good reasons to affirm. First, we were made for eternity. Second, we are free-willed moral agents, and always will be. Third, God is just. There is a place for those who say "Yes" to him and a place for those who say "No," and no one ends up in the wrong place. Fourth, because God is just, it is not the case, as some object, that hell is an eternal punishment for temporal sin. Hell's inhabitants continue to reject God throughout eternity. Hell is an outpost of rebellion against God, and its inhabitants are "successful rebels to the end." (See C.S. Lewis: "I willingly believe that the damned are, in one sense successful rebels to the end; that the doors of hell are locked from the inside." C.S. Lewis, *The Problem of Pain*, p. 130.)

Fifth, because God is just, the nature and intensity of pain and suffering in hell is no more, no less, and nothing other than, the actual consequences of a sinner's choice to live apart from God. Sixth, we are all moving toward heaven or hell even now. As C.S. Lewis put it:

> Every time you make a choice, you are turning the central part of you, the part that chooses, into something a little different from what was before...you are slowly turning this central thing either into a heavenly creature or a hellish creature...to be one kind of creature is heaven; that is joy and peace and knowledge and power. To be the other means madness, horror, idiocy, rage, impotence, and eternal loneliness. Each of us at each moment is progressing to one state or the other.

C.S. Lewis, *Mere Christianity* (New York: Simon & Schuster. Touchstone Edition, 1996), p. 92.

Finally, God is true to his promise: "You will seek me and find me when you seek me with all your heart." No one who seeks God in this way will fail to find him and their heart's satisfaction in him. Hell is a problem, but one that can be avoided.

[9] There are two views, each held by some Christians, which do not include hell as an ongoing, eternal state of affairs. The first is annihilationism, the belief that those who are not bound for heaven will simply cease to exist with their last breath. Hell, according to this view, is a metaphor for the finality of death. The second is view universalism, the belief that in time hell will be vacated as the love of God triumphs in human hearts and heaven is embraced freely and fully. I don't believe that either of these views squares with the biblical witness.

[10] See Psalm 16:11:

> You make known to me the path of life;
>   in your presence there is fullness of joy;
>   at your right hand are pleasures forevermore.

[11] "The Lord is not slow to fulfill his promise as some count slowness, but is patient toward you, not wishing that any should perish, but that all should reach repentance." (2 Peter 3:9)

¹² That is, everything that happens serves the interests of the glory of God. It is a means to that greater end.

¹³ Believers say that *some* pain and suffering is judicially related to God. As the state punishes wrongdoers, with the result that their pain and suffering is just, so God magnifies his justice through the punishment of sin, whether it is served indirectly through moral agents or natural forces, or directly by him. The greater good served in such instances is the glory of a holy and just God.

¹⁴ Karl Barth, *Church Dogmatics*, eds., Geoffrey W. Bromiley, T. F. Torrance (New York: Charles Scribner's Sons, 1957), Vol. II, pp. 647, 653, 655. As C.S. Lewis saw it, "Fully to enjoy is to glorify. In commanding us to glorify Him, God is inviting us to enjoy Him." C.S. Lewis, *Reflections on the Psalms* (New York: Harcourt Brace Jovanovich, 1958), p. 97.

¹⁵ In his work, *The Problem of Pain*, C.S. Lewis introduced us to the distinction between a simple good, a simple evil, and a complex good. He wrote:

> Suffering is not good in itself. What is good in any painful experience is, for the sufferer, his submission to the will of God, and, for the spectators, the compassion aroused and the acts of mercy to which it leads. In the fallen and partially redeemed universe we may distinguish (1) The simple good descending from God, (2) The simple evil produced by rebellious creatures, and (3) the exploitation of that evil by God for His redemptive purpose, which produces (4) the complex good to which accepted suffering and repented sin contribute.

C.S. Lewis, *The Problem of Pain*, pp. 110-111.

¹⁶ See:

> I am the LORD who practices steadfast love, justice and righteousness in the earth; *for in these things I delight*, says the LORD. (Jeremiah 9:24, RSV)

> Who is a God like you, pardoning iniquity
>   and passing over the transgression
>   for the remnant of his inheritance?
> He does not retain his anger forever
>   because *he delights* in steadfast love. (Micah 7:18)

¹⁷ Jesus perfectly embodied this virtue and this joy, which is why he could say to his followers: "If you keep my commandments, you will abide in my love, just as I have kept my Father's commandments and abide in his love. These things I have spoken to you, that my joy may be in you, and that your joy may be full." (John 15:10-11)

¹⁸ "But now you must put them all away: anger, wrath, malice, slander, and obscene talk from your mouth. Do not lie to one another, seeing that you have put off the old self with its practices and have put on the new self, which is being renewed in knowledge after the image of its creator." (Colossians 3:8-10)

¹⁹ Although it does not focus explicitly on what God is doing in the midst human suffering, pain, and evil in the world, the comprehensive language used by the apostle Paul in his letter to the church in Rome includes these things:

> And we know that for those who love God all things work together for good, for those who are called according to his purpose. For those whom he foreknew he also predestined to be conformed to the image of his Son, in order that he might be the firstborn among many brothers. (Romans 8:28-29)

There are three important observations to make about this passage. First, the "good" in view is contingently related to loving God and a calling that aligns with the purposes of God. Second, if we ask what this "good" is, the context suggests that it has to do with people becoming like Christ ("conformed to the image of his Son"). Third, the language of predestination invites us to put these issues into an eternal framework in the purposes of God.

²⁰ "But according to his promise we are waiting for new heavens and a new earth in which righteousness dwells." (2 Peter 3:13)

²¹ This notion goes back to the Church Fathers, Irenaeus and Origen, who saw humans as incomplete and imperfect, and saw the world as an environment designed by God for their moral and spiritual development, with the challenges of pain and suffering as an essential component in their growth.

See the development of this theme in John Hick, *Evil and the God of Love* rev. ed. (San Francisco: Harper & Row, 1978). See also R. Douglas Geivett, *Evil and the Evidence for God: The Challenge of John Hick's Theodicy* (Philadelphia, PA: Temple University Press, 1995).

People whose souls are being shaped well flourish in joy, whatever life may bring. They embrace the Creator's mandate to fulfill his vision for the world and the human project. They steward the resources of the world as an expression of love for its Maker and love for their neighbors. They are fruitful in the righteousness, peace, and joy of God's Kingdom.

²² God's gift of moral freedom is a necessary condition for joy. Without moral freedom we are not responsible for our beliefs, our values, our actions, or the development of our character – all of which are essential for joy. Unless we can say a meaningful "Yes" to God, the joy for which we were created is an empty abstraction. It comes to life in our flesh-and-bones existence when we offer God's gift of freedom back to him, when our hearts affirm, embrace, and treasure his purposes for our lives, and we do this freely. Moral freedom creates the possibility of evil in the world, but it also makes our greatest good possible. We can't have one without the other.

²³ We see this played out, for instance, in Hebrews 11, where faith is defined as "the assurance of things hoped for, the conviction of things not seen" (v. 2), we are told that "without faith it is impossible to please [God], for whoever would draw near to God must believe that he exists and that he rewards those who seek him" (v. 6) and we are

then shown a parade of men and women in the Jewish Scriptures who exemplified this faith (verses 7 and following).

24 Matthew 25:21, 23

25 2 Corinthians 4:17

26 For a development of this theme, see Marilyn McCord Adams, *Horrendous Evils and the Goodness of God* (Ithaca, NY: Cornell University Press, 1999).

27 See Leibniz, *Theodicy*.

28 If you are not familiar with the words *eschaton* or *eschatological*, they refer to what Christians call the "last days" or "end times."

29 See John Piper, *A Godward Life: Savoring the Supremacy of God in All of Life* (Colorado Springs, Colorado: Multnomah, First Edition 1997; New Edition 2001; New Hardcover 2015).

30 Romans 15:13

31 Karl Barth wrote, "Most joy is anticipatory. Even in the experience of the fulfillment, and particularly when this experience is genuine, it usually changes immediately into anticipatory joy, i.e., joy in expectation of further fulfillment. In this respect, it normally has something of an eschatological character." Karl Barth, *Church Dogmatics*, Vol. III, Part 4, p. 377.

32 Featured in the Lord's Prayer:

> Our Father in heaven,
>   hallowed be your name.
> Your Kingdom come,
>   your will be done,
>   on earth as it is in heaven.
> Give us this day our daily bread,
>   and forgive us our debts,
>   as we also have forgiven our debtors.
> And lead us not into temptation,
>   but deliver us from evil.
> For yours is the Kingdom, the power and glory, forever. Amen.
> (Matthew 6:9-13, with traditional ending)

33 I am indebted to George Eldon Ladd for this insight. See his work, *A Theology of the New Testament* (Grand Rapids: William B. Eerdmans Publishing Co., 1974).

34 A play on words from Tolkien's description of what he calls *eucatastrophe*:

> The eucatastrophic tale is the true form of fairy-tale, and its highest function . . . . It does not deny the existence of *dyscatastrophe*, of sorrow and failure: the possibility of these is necessary to the joy of deliverance; it denies . . . universal final defeat and in so

far is *evangelium,* giving a fleeting glimpse of Joy, Joy beyond the walls of the world, poignant as grief . . . . In such stories . . . we get a piercing glimpse of joy, and heart's desire, that for a moment passes outside the frame, *rends indeed the very web of story, and lets a gleam come through.*

J.R.R. Tolkien, *The Tolkien Reader* (New York: Ballentine Books, 1966), pp. 86-87. (Emphasis in final phrase added.)

[35] C.S. Lewis, *Mere Christianity,* p. 153.

[36] Acts 17:27-28

[37] Augustine, "Confessions" in *The Works of Saint Augustine: A Translation for the 21ˢᵗ Century,* ed. John E. Rotelle, trans. Maria Boulding (New York: New City Press, 1997), I/1, p. 83.

[38] See:

> Where shall I go from your Spirit?
>> Or where shall I flee from your presence?
> If I ascend to heaven, you are there!
>> If I make my bed in Sheol, you are there!
> If I take the wings of the morning
>> and dwell in the uttermost parts of the sea,
> even there your hand shall lead me,
>> and your right hand shall hold me.
> If I say, 'Surely the darkness shall cover me,
>> and the light about me be night,'
> even the darkness is not dark to you;
>> the night is bright as the day,
>> for darkness is as light with you. (Psalm 139:7-12)

[39] You can start your meditation with Scriptures like these:

> Yet he is not far from each one of us, for "in him we live and move and have our being." (Acts 17:28, RSV)

> Even though I walk through the valley of the shadow of death,
>> I will fear no evil,
> for you are with me;
>> your rod and your staff,
>> they comfort me. (Psalm 23:4)

> "God is our refuge and strength,
>> a very present help in trouble." (Psalm 46:1)

> Where shall I go from your Spirit?
>> Or where shall I flee from your presence?
> If I ascend to heaven, you are there!
>> If I make my bed in Sheol, you are there!
> If I take the wings of the morning
>> and dwell in the uttermost parts of the sea,
> even there your hand shall lead me,

and your right hand shall hold me. (Psalm 139:7-10)

Fear not, for I have redeemed you;
  I have called you by name; you are mine.
When you pass through the waters, I will be with you;
  and through the rivers, they shall not overwhelm you;
when you walk through fire you shall not be burned,
  and the flame shall not consume you . . .
Fear not, for I am with you. (Isaiah 43:1-5)

40 "I have set the LORD always before me;
      because he is at my right hand, I shall not be shaken. (Psalm 16:8)

41 "My eyes are ever toward the LORD." (Psalm 25:15)

42 Psalm 73:28

43 See the following:

Teach me your way, O LORD, that I may walk in your truth. (Psalm 86:11)

I have no greater joy than to hear that my children are walking in the truth. (3 John 1:4)

44 See the following:

For those whom he foreknew he also predestined to be conformed to the image of his Son, in order that he might be the firstborn among many brothers. (Romans 8:29)

And we all, with unveiled face, beholding the glory of the Lord, are being transformed into the same image from one degree of glory to another. For this comes from the Lord who is the Spirit. (2 Corinthians 3:18)

45 See the following:

In these last days [God] has spoken to us by his Son, whom he appointed the heir of all things, through whom also he created the world. He is the radiance of the glory of God and the exact imprint of his nature. (Hebrews 1:2-3)

For those whom he foreknew he also predestined to be conformed to the image of his Son, in order that he might be the first-born among many brethren. (Romans 8:29)

My little children, with whom I am again in travail until Christ be formed in you! (Galatians 4:19)

. . . until we all attain to the unity of the faith and of the knowledge of the Son of God, to mature manhood, to the measure of the stature of the fulness of Christ. (Ephesians 4:13)

46 John 15:11

CHAPTER 5: JOY AND THE KINGDOM OF GOD

[1] The content of this chapter is drawn largely from earlier writings of mine on joy, including Chapter 12 in Rick Howe, *Path of Life: Finding the Joy You've Always Longed For* (Boulder, CO: University Ministries Press, Revised Edition, 2017) and Chapters 14 and 15 in Rick Howe, *River of Delights: Quenching Your Thirst For Joy*, Volume 2 (Boulder, CO: University Ministries Press, Revised Editions, 2017).

[2] Ours is a narcissistic age. Christopher Lasch described it this way:

> After the political turmoil of the sixties, Americans have retreated to purely personal preoccupations. Having no hope of improving their lives in any of the ways that matter, people have convinced themselves that what matters is psychic self-improvement: getting in touch with their feelings, eating health food, taking lessons in ballet or belly-dancing, immersing themselves in the wisdom of the East, jogging, learning how to "relate," overcoming the "fear of pleasure."

> The contemporary climate is therapeutic, not religious. People today hunger not for personal satisfaction, let alone for the restoration of an earlier age, but for the feeling, the momentary illusion, of personal well-being, health and psychic security.

Christopher Lasch, *The Culture of Narcissism* (New York: Norton, 1978), pp. 4, 7.

Writing two years earlier, Francis Schaeffer warned that the United States, on the heels of its European forebears, had entered a post-Christian era. Values and convictions that once held our culture together no longer did. All that remained of Christianity for many were memories without power, words without meaning, and rituals without reality. He saw frightening portents of what might lie ahead and sounded a prophetic alarm. What he saw, to his dismay, was that many who bore the name of Christ had slowly, quietly, and uncritically come to embrace cultural values that were seriously at odds with Christ and his ways. Chief among them were personal peace and affluence. See Francis A. Schaeffer, *How Should We Then Live? The Rise and Decline of Western Thought and Culture* (Old Tappan, New Jersey: Fleming H. Revell Company, 1976), p. 205ff.

In the same year, Paul Tournier wrote of Christians:

> What I am concerned about are the large numbers of people who are victims of a tragic misunderstanding. They take no further interest in worldly matters because their interest has – quite properly – been awakened in regard to the spiritual verities, as if the latter could exist in themselves in the abstract, outside of their incarnation in the world.

Paul Tournier, *The Adventure of Living* (New York: Harper & Row, 1976), p. 202.

[3] I wrote in *Path of Life*:

> Joy engages us as subjects, but it is never merely subjective. It is the enjoyment of someone or something. It always has an outward look. It is always attached. In this sense, there is no such thing as joy in itself. You can't extract joy, as you might cinnamon from a cinnamon tree, and then enjoy the taste in itself. Joy is governed by its objects.

Joy must always be hyphenated in our thinking. It is always joy-in-God or joy-in-his-gifts or joy-in-our-neighbors. Joy in God's creation, for instance, is our pleasure in a rainbow or the song of a nightingale. Joy may linger beyond the encounter, and may even return in memory; it is still, however, attached to an object. . . .

You will never find joy by looking for it in itself. It is always found in an outward look, in an engagement with God, his world, and the people he has created. It can't be found anywhere else.

Rick Howe, *Path of Life: Finding the Joy You've Always Longed For* (Boulder, CO: University Ministries Press, Revised Edition 2017), p. 152.

[4] Quoted in see William Morrice, *Joy in the New Testament* (Grand Rapids, Michigan: Eerdmans, 1984), p. 107.

[5] The highest praise we give a sacrificial act done for another is to say that it was a joy to do it. We see this in the language used to describe Jesus and his redemptive act on the cross: ". . . looking to Jesus, the founder and perfecter of our faith, who for the joy that was set before him endured the cross, despising the shame. . . ." (Hebrews 12:2)

[6] Though many have forgotten, this has been central to the Christian story from its opening chapter. Jesus taught his disciples to face adversity with joy: "Blessed are you when men revile you and persecute you and utter all kinds of evil against you on my account. Rejoice and be glad." (Matthew 5:11-12a) When persecution came, his followers responded with joy "that they were counted worthy to suffer dishonor" for Christ. (Acts 5:41) Paul wrote, "I rejoice in my sufferings." (Colossians 1:24) James exhorted his audience, "Count it all joy, my brothers, when you meet trials of various kinds." (James 1:2) Peter approached life the same way: "Rejoice in so far as you share Christ's sufferings." (1 Peter 4:13)

[7] Mark 1:15

[8] See:

> The Spirit of the LORD God is upon me,
>   because the LORD has anointed me
> to bring good news to the poor;
>   he has sent me to bind up the brokenhearted,
> to proclaim liberty to the captives,
>   and the opening of the prison to those who are bound;
> to proclaim the year of the LORD's favor,
>   and the day of vengeance of our God;
>   to comfort all who mourn. (Isaiah 61:1-2)

[9] With traditional ending.

[10] "From that time Jesus began to preach, saying, 'Repent, for the kingdom of heaven is at hand.' . . . And he went throughout all Galilee, teaching in their synagogues and proclaiming the gospel of the kingdom and healing every disease and every affliction among the people." (Matthew 4:17, 23)

11   See, for example, the Sermon on the Mount:

> Blessed are the poor in spirit, for theirs is the kingdom of heaven. (Matthew 5:3)

> Blessed are those who are persecuted for righteousness' sake, for theirs is the kingdom of heaven. (Matthew 5:10)

> For I tell you, unless your righteousness exceeds that of the scribes and Pharisees, you will never enter the kingdom of heaven. (Matthew 5:20)

> Your kingdom come, your will be done, on earth as it is in heaven. (Matthew 6:10)

> For yours is the kingdom and the power and the glory, forever. Amen (Matthew 6:13)

> But seek first the kingdom of God and his righteousness, and all these things will be added to you. (Matthew 6:33)

> Not everyone who says to me, "Lord, Lord," will enter the kingdom of heaven, but the one who does the will of my Father who is in heaven. (Matthew 7:21)

12   See, for example, Jesus' parables of the Kingdom in Matthew 13.

13   See:

> And if I cast out demons by Beelzebul, by whom do your sons cast them out? Therefore they will be your judges. But if it is by the Spirit of God that I cast out demons, then the kingdom of God has come upon you. Or how can someone enter a strong man's house and plunder his goods, unless he first binds the strong man? Then indeed he may plunder his house. (Matthew 12:27-29)

14   Compare:

> But if it is by the Spirit of God that I cast out demons, then the kingdom of God has come upon you.   (Matthew 12:28)

> But if it is by the finger of God that I cast out demons, then the kingdom of God has come upon you. (Luke 11:20)

15   See the following:

> And he called the twelve together and gave them power and authority over all demons and to cure diseases, and he sent them out to proclaim the kingdom of God and to heal. And he said to them, "Take nothing for your journey, no staff, nor bag, nor bread, nor money; and do not have two tunics. And whatever house you enter, stay there, and from there depart. And wherever they do not receive you, when you leave that town shake off the dust from your feet as a testimony against them." And they departed and went through the villages, preaching the gospel and healing everywhere. (Luke 9:1-6)

> After this the Lord appointed seventy-two others and sent them on ahead of him, two by two, into every town and place where he himself was about to go. And he said to them, "The harvest is plentiful, but the laborers are few. Therefore pray earnestly to the Lord of the harvest to send out laborers into his harvest. Go your way; behold, I am sending you out as lambs in the midst of wolves. Carry no moneybag, no knapsack, no

sandals, and greet no one on the road. Whatever house you enter, first say, 'Peace be to this house!' And if a son of peace is there, your peace will rest upon him. But if not, it will return to you. And remain in the same house, eating and drinking what they provide, for the laborer deserves his wages. Do not go from house to house. Whenever you enter a town and they receive you, eat what is set before you. Heal the sick in it and say to them, 'The kingdom of God has come near to you.' But whenever you enter a town and they do not receive you, go into its streets and say, 'Even the dust of your town that clings to our feet we wipe off against you. Nevertheless know this, that the kingdom of God has come near.' I tell you, it will be more bearable on that day for Sodom than for that town. (Luke 10:1-12)

16   "And this gospel of the kingdom will be proclaimed throughout the whole world as a testimony to all nations, and then the end will come." (Matthew 24:14)

17   "And I tell you, you are Peter, and on this rock I will build my church, and the gates of hell shall not prevail against it. I will give you the keys of the kingdom of heaven, and whatever you bind on earth shall be bound in heaven, and whatever you loose on earth shall be loosed in heaven." (Matthew 16:18-19)

18   "He presented himself alive to them after his suffering by many proofs, appearing to them during forty days and speaking about the kingdom of God." (Acts 1:3)

19   "For the kingdom of God is not a matter of eating and drinking but of righteousness and peace and joy in the Holy Spirit." (Romans 14:17)

20   Many passages speak of the Kingdom as yet future. See for example:

Your kingdom come, your will be done, on earth as it is in heaven. (Matthew. 6:10)

Then the King will say to those on his right, 'Come, you who are blessed by my Father, inherit the kingdom prepared for you from the foundation of the world. (Matthew 25:34)

Then he left the crowds and went into the house. And his disciples came to him, saying, "Explain to us the parable of the weeds of the field." He answered, "The one who sows the good seed is the Son of Man. The field is the world, and the good seed is the sons of the kingdom. The weeds are the sons of the evil one, and the enemy who sowed them is the devil. The harvest is the end of the age, and the reapers are angels. Just as the weeds are gathered and burned with fire, so will it be at the end of the age. The Son of Man will send his angels, and they will gather out of his kingdom all causes of sin and all law-breakers, and throw them into the fiery furnace. In that place there will be weeping and gnashing of teeth. Then the righteous will shine like the sun in the kingdom of their Father. He who has ears, let him hear. (Matthew 13:36-43)

In that place there will be weeping and gnashing of teeth, when you see Abraham and Isaac and Jacob and all the prophets in the kingdom of God but you yourselves cast out. And people will come from east and west, and from north and south, and recline at table in the kingdom of God. (Luke 13:28-29)

21   Philippians 2:11

22   I rely heavily on the scholarly work of George Eldon Ladd on the Kingdom of God in the New Testament. See George Eldon Ladd, *A Theology of the New Testament* (Grand Rapids, MI: William B. Eerdmans Publishing Co., revised 1993), chapters 4-9.

23   There are also many passages that speak of the Kingdom as a present reality. See, for example:

> Blessed are the poor in spirit, for theirs is the kingdom of heaven. (Matthew 5:3)

> Blessed are those who are persecuted for righteousness' sake, for theirs is the kingdom of heaven (Matthew 5:10)

> But seek first the kingdom of God and his righteousness, and all these things will be added to you. (Matthew 6:33)

> Truly, I say to you, among those born of women there has arisen no one greater than John the Baptist. Yet the one who is least in the kingdom of heaven is greater than he. From the days of John the Baptist until now the kingdom of heaven has suffered violence, and the violent take it by force. For all the Prophets and the Law prophesied until John. (Matthew 11:11-13)

> But if it is by the Spirit of God that I cast out demons, then the kingdom of God has come upon you. (Matthew 12:28)

> Which of the two did the will of his father?" They said, "The first." Jesus said to them, "Truly, I say to you, the tax collectors and the prostitutes go into the kingdom of God before you. (Matthew 21:31)

> But woe to you, scribes and Pharisees, hypocrites! For you shut the kingdom of heaven in people's faces. For you neither enter yourselves nor allow those who would enter to go in.   (Matthew 23:13)

> The time is fulfilled, and the kingdom of God is at hand; repent and believe in the gospel. (Mark 1:15)

> But when Jesus saw it, he was indignant and said to them, "Let the children come to me; do not hinder them, for to such belongs the kingdom of God. Truly, I say to you, whoever does not receive the kingdom of God like a child shall not enter it."   (Mark 10:14-15)

> Being asked by the Pharisees when the kingdom of God would come, he answered them, "The kingdom of God is not coming in ways that can be observed." (Luke 17:20)

24   See, for example:

> For I tell you, unless your righteousness exceeds that of the scribes and Pharisees, you will never enter the kingdom of heaven. (Matthew 5:20)

> Not everyone who says to me, 'Lord, Lord,' will enter the kingdom of heaven, but the one who does the will of my Father who is in heaven. (Matthew 7:21)

Truly, I say to you, unless you turn and become like children, you will never enter the kingdom of heaven. (Matthew 18:3)

Truly, I say to you, only with difficulty will a rich person enter the kingdom of heaven. (Matthew 19:23)

But woe to you, scribes and Pharisees, hypocrites! For you shut the kingdom of heaven in people's faces. For you neither enter yourselves nor allow those who would enter to go in. (Matthew 23:13)

[25] Mark 1:14-15

[26] The Greek word for repentance, *metanoia*, literally means a "change of mind." Gerhard Kittel, ed., *Theological Dictionary of the New Testament*, trans. Geoffrey W. Bromiley (Grand Rapids, MI: Wm. B. Eerdmans Publishing Co., 1964), Vol. IV, p. 978. It is a radical change of mind and change of heart that leads to a change in direction and a changed life.

[27] You can read the parable in full in Luke 15:11-32.

[28] See:

For not only has the word of the Lord sounded forth from you in Macedonia and Achaia, but your faith in God has gone forth everywhere, so that we need not say anything. For they themselves report concerning us the kind of reception we had among you, and how you turned to God from idols to serve *the living and true God.*" (1 Thessalonians 1:8-9)

[29] C.S. Lewis, *Reflections on the Psalms* (New York: Harcourt Brace Jovanovich, 1958) p. 32.

It is true that the Scriptures sometimes speak of God's hatred of sinners (e.g., Psalm 5:4-6), but, in light of other clear statements about God's love for sinners, we should interpret those passages to mean that he hates the wicked *with respect to* their wickedness, the evil *with respect to* their evil, and sinners *with respect to* their sin.

C.S. Lewis wrote:

I remember Christian teachers telling me long ago that I must hate a bad man's actions, but not hate the bad man: or, as they would say, hate the sin but not the sinner.

For a long time I used to think this a silly, straw-splitting distinction: how could you hate what a man did and not hate the man? But years later it occurred to me that there was one man to whom I had been doing this all my life—namely myself. However much I might dislike my own cowardice or conceit or greed, I went on loving myself. There had never been the slightest difficulty about it. In fact the very reason why I hated the things was that I loved the man. Just because I loved myself, I was sorry to find that I was the sort of man who did those things. Consequently, Christianity does not want us to reduce by one atom the hatred we feel for cruelty and treachery. We ought to hate them. Not one word of what we have said about them needs to be unsaid. But it does want us to hate them in the same way in which we hate things in ourselves:

being sorry that the man should have done such things, and hoping, if it is anyway possible, that somehow, sometime, somewhere he can be cured and made human again.

C.S. Lewis, *Mere Christianity* (New York: Harper Collins, 2001), p. 117.

[30] Luther's Ninety-five Theses began with this assertion: "When our Lord and Master Jesus Christ said 'Repent,' he intended that the entire life of believers should be repentance." See *Luther's Works*, ed., Harold J. Grim, (Philadelphia: Muhlenberg Press, 1957), Vol. 31, p. 25.

[31] The apostle Paul contrasts those whose sin keeps them from the Kingdom of God with those in whom the fruit of the Spirit grows:

> Now the works of the flesh are evident: sexual immorality, impurity, sensuality, idolatry, sorcery, enmity, strife, jealousy, fits of anger, rivalries, dissensions, divisions, envy, drunkenness, orgies, and things like these. I warn you, as I warned you before, *that those who do such things will not inherit the kingdom of God. But the fruit of the Spirit is love, joy, peace, patience, kindness, goodness, faithfulness, gentleness, self-control*; against such things there is no law. (Galatians 5:19-23)

[32] Romans 14:17, RSV

[33] This is taught vividly in the story of Joshua before the gates of Jericho:

> When Joshua was by Jericho, he lifted up his eyes and looked, and behold, a man was standing before him with his drawn sword in his hand. And Joshua went to him and said to him, "Are you for us, or for our adversaries?" And he said, "No; but I am the commander of the army of the LORD. Now I have come." And Joshua fell on his face to the earth and worshiped and said to him, "What does my lord say to his servant?" And the commander of the LORD's army said to Joshua, "Take off your sandals from your feet, for the place where you are standing is holy." And Joshua did so. (Joshua 5:13-15).

[34] Romans 14:18, literal translation.

[35] C.K. Barrett, *A Commentary on the Epistle to the Romans* (New York: Harper & Row Publishers, 1957), p. 265.

Kingdom righteousness in this context is not "the status of righteousness before God which is God's gift." C.E.B. Cranfield, *A Critical and Exegetical Commentary on The Epistle to the Romans* (Edinburgh: T&T Clark Limited, 1979, reprint. 1981), Vol. 2, p. 718. If we let Paul speak for himself, and speak his mind fully, he sees righteousness both as a judicial standing before God, and as action that seeks the well-being of others before God. The first is his doctrine of justification ("righteousness by faith") and is especially in view in chapters 3-5 of his letter to the Romans. The second is a "righteousness leading to sanctification" (e.g., Romans 6:13, 16, 18, 19), and includes the many practical exhortations that seek the good of others in Romans 12-14.

[36] See the following:

For I have chosen him, that he may command his children and his household after him to keep the way of the LORD by *doing righteousness* and justice, so that the Lord may bring to Abraham what he has promised him." (Genesis 18:19)

Blessed are they who observe justice, who *do righteousness* at all times! (Psalm 106:3)

To *do righteousness* and justice is more acceptable to the LORD than sacrifice. (Proverbs 21:3)

Thus says the LORD: "Keep justice, and *do righteousness*, for soon my salvation will come, and my righteousness be revealed. (Isaiah 56:1)
Thus says the LORD: *Do justice and righteousness*, and deliver from the hand of the oppressor him who has been robbed. (Jeremiah 22:3)

[37]   Contextually, Paul is concerned with those who "put a stumbling block or hindrance in the way of a brother" (14:13, RSV). If righteousness is action taken to help others flourish before God, then acting in ways that cause others to fall is a direct contradiction to this. The positive commitment to righteousness in this sense is found, for instance, in 14:19 – "Let us then pursue what makes for peace and for mutual up building," (RSV) and in 15:2, "Let each of us please his neighbor for his good, to edify him." (RSV)

[38]   Psalm 97:2

[39]   From the beginning of the human project, God exercises dominion in developing the world through human agents. This is true of the "cultural mandate" given in creation, and it is true in our era of the Kingdom.

[40]   See also:

I delivered the poor who cried,
and the fatherless who had none to help him.
The blessing of him who was about to perish came upon me,
and I caused the widow's heart to sing for joy.
I put on righteousness, and it clothed me;
my justice was like a robe and a turban.
I was eyes to the blind,
and feet to the lame.
I was a father to the poor,
and I searched out the cause of him whom I did not know.
I broke the fangs of the unrighteous,
and made him drop his prey from his teeth." (Job 29:12-17, RSV)

The righteous care about justice for the poor. (Proverbs 29:7, NIV)

Then the righteous will answer him, "Lord, when did we see you hungry and feed you, or thirsty and give you something to drink? When did we see you a stranger and invite you in, or needing clothes and clothe you? When did we see you sick or in prison and go to visit you?" The King will reply, "I tell you the truth, whatever you did for one of the least of these brothers of mine, you did for me." (Matthew 25:37-40, NIV)

[41]   Joy is both a centrifugal and a centripetal spiritual force: It reaches out and draws others in. Joy is hospitable: always seeking company and inviting and bringing others home to

share its boon. Our own joy is enhanced, enriched, and enlarged as we give ourselves to its largess. James Gilman puts this into the context of our concern for the poor, "The community's joy lies in the privilege of sharing with the poor the same gracious kindness it receives from God, so that in the end both donor and recipient rejoice together." James E. Gilman, *Fidelity of the Heart, An Ethic of Christian Virtue* (Oxford: Oxford University Press, 2001), p. 61.

[42] The biblical concepts of righteousness and justice overlap. Biblical justice is not the same as the classical Greek understanding of this moral quality. In its Aristotelian sense, justice is calculating and disinterested. It is giving a person his due. From a biblical perspective the just person is not merely one who acts justly because it is required of him; he desires justice, loves justice, and delights in justice. It is not disinterested or detached, but passionately involved. It is not giving a person his due on the basis of merit, but acting in ways that will promote human flourishing as an expression of love.

[43] See his teaching on this matter recorded in Matthew 25:31-40:

> When the Son of Man comes in his glory, and all the angels with him, then he will sit on his glorious throne. Before him will be gathered all the nations, and he will separate people one from another as a shepherd separates the sheep from the goats. And he will place the sheep on his right, but the goats on the left. Then the King will say to those on his right, "Come, you who are blessed by my Father, inherit the kingdom prepared for you from the foundation of the world. For I was hungry and you gave me food, I was thirsty and you gave me drink, I was a stranger and you welcomed me, I was naked and you clothed me, I was sick and you visited me, I was in prison and you came to me." Then the righteous will answer him, saying, "Lord, when did we see you hungry and feed you, or thirsty and give you drink? And when did we see you a stranger and welcome you, or naked and clothe you? And when did we see you sick or in prison and visit you?" And the King will answer them, "Truly, I say to you, as you did it to one of the least of these my brothers, you did it to me."

[44] Though they are related, and outwardly may appear to be the same, it is important to say here that kingdom righteousness is not an equivalent term for social justice. Donald Bloesch writes:

> Both humanitarian works of mercy and works of social reform are at best approximations of kingdom righteousness. If the church identified itself with the cause of social justice, this might indeed make people more receptive to the kingdom message. Social justice is a partial fulfillment of the law of God; the eschatological kingdom is the perfect fulfillment of the teachings of the law. Social justice is related to the law of God; the righteousness of the kingdom is related to the gospel. Social justice is conducive to human happiness; Christian obedience brings blessedness – contagious, radiant joy.

Donald G. Bloesch, *Freedom for Obedience: Evangelical Ethics in Contemporary Times* (San Francisco: Harper and Row, 1987), p. 84.

[45] "Have no anxiety about anything, but in everything by prayer and supplication with thanksgiving let your requests be made known to God. And the peace of God, which passes all understanding, will keep your hearts and your minds in Christ Jesus." (Philippians 4:6-7, RSV)

46   "Let us then pursue what makes for peace and for mutual upbuilding." (Romans 14:19, RSV)

47   Romans 12:18

48   *Shalom* is a prominent theme in Isaiah:

> For to us a child is born,
>   to us a son is given;
> and the government shall be upon his shoulder,
>   and his name shall be called
> Wonderful Counselor, Mighty God,
>   Everlasting Father, Prince of *Peace*.
> Of the increase of his government and of *peace*
>   there will be no end,
> on the throne of David and over his kingdom,
>   to establish it and to uphold it
> with justice and with righteousness
>   from this time forth and forevermore.
> The zeal of the LORD of hosts will do this. (9:6-7)

> You keep him in perfect *peace*
>   whose mind is stayed on you,
> because he trusts in you. (26:1)

> O LORD, you will ordain *peace* for us,
>   for you have indeed done for us all our works. (26:12)

> And the effect of righteousness will be *peace*,
>   and the result of righteousness, quietness and trust forever.
> My people will abide in a *peaceful* habitation,
>   in secure dwellings, and in quiet resting places. (32:17-18)

> Oh that you had paid attention to my commandments!
> Then your *peace* would have been like a river,
>   and your righteousness like the waves of the sea; (48:18)

> How beautiful upon the mountains
>   are the feet of him who brings good news,
> who publishes *peace*, who brings good news of happiness,
>   who publishes salvation,
>   who says to Zion, "Your God reigns." (52:7)

> For the mountains may depart
>   and the hills be removed,
> but my steadfast love shall not depart from you,
>   and my covenant of *peace* shall not be removed,"
>   says the LORD, who has compassion on you. (54:10)

> "For you shall go out in joy
>   and be led forth in *peace*;
> the mountains and the hills before you
>   shall break forth into singing,
>   and all the trees of the field shall clap their hands. (55:12)

I have seen his ways, but I will heal him;
    I will lead him and restore comfort to him and his mourners,
    creating the fruit of the lips.
Peace, peace, to the far and to the near," says the LORD,
    "and I will heal him. (57:18-19)

[49] Cornelius Plantinga, Jr., *Not the Way It's Supposed to Be: A Breviary of Sin*, (Grand Rapids, MI: William B. Eerdmans Publishing Company, 1995), p.10.

[50] "Healthy joy cannot be full while sisters and brothers are in misery. Joy in a surrounding context of misery is insulted and undone." Daniel C. Maguire, *The Moral Core of Judaism and Christianity: Reclaiming the Revolution* (Minneapolis: Fortress Press, 1993), p. 279.

[51] See Isaiah 32:17-18.

> And *the effect of righteousness will be peace*,
>   and the result of righteousness, quietness and trust forever.
> My people will abide in a peaceful habitation,
>   in secure dwellings, and in quiet resting places.

[52] "Joy is what humans experience when the way the world is and the way the world ought to be converge. For Christians joy is love's delight in God and God's promised kingdom, when the way the world is and the way God wills the world converge." Gilman, *Fidelity of Heart:* p. 54.

[53] In this context, joy as the consummation of *shalom*:

> It is "the fulfillment of our capacity for rejoicing." Maguire, *Moral Core*, p. 236.

> It is to "enjoy living before God, to enjoy living in nature, to enjoy living with one's fellows, to enjoy life with oneself." Nicholas Wolterstorff, *Art in Action: Toward a Christian Aesthetic* (Grand Rapids: Eerdmans, 1980), p. 79.

> It is "a just peace with joy in God's creation." Donald G. Bloesch, *Freedom for Obedience: Evangelical Ethics in Contemporary Times* (San Francisco: Harper and Row, 1987), p. 90.

[54] Cornelius Plantinga writes:

> The prophets knew how many ways human life can go wrong because they knew how many ways human life can go right. (You need the concept of a wall on a plumb to tell when one is off.) These prophets kept dreaming of a time when God would put things right again.

> They dreamed of a new age in which human crookedness would be straightened out, rough places made plain. The foolish would be made wise and the wise, humble. They dreamed of a time when the deserts would flower, the mountains would run with wine, weeping would cease and people could go to sleep without weapons on their laps. People would work in peace and work to fruitful effect. Lambs could lie down with lions. All nature would be fruitful, benign, and filled with wonder upon wonder; all humans would be knit together in brotherhood and sisterhood; and all nature and all

humans would look to God, walk with God, lean toward God and delight in God. Shouts of joy and recognition would well up from valleys and seas, from women in streets and from men on ships.

Cornelius Plantinga, Jr., Ibid.

[55] This is the joy which Madeleine L'Engle sees captured in the Sanskrit word, *ananda*: that joy in existence, without which the universe will fall apart and collapse." Madeleine L'Engle, *A Swiftly Tilting Planet* (New York, NY: Dell Publishing, 1979), p. 40. It is the joy that binds Being to being, and all created things to each other. It is the aim of creation and redemption alike.

John Calvin wrote:

> [The] Psalmist calls upon irrational things themselves, the trees, the earth, the seas, and the heavens, to join in the general joy. Nor are we to understand that by the heavens he means the angels, and by the earth men; for he calls even upon the dumb fishes of the deep to shout for joy. . . . As all elements in the creation groan and travail together with us, according to Paul's declaration, (Rom. 8:22) they may reasonably rejoice in the restoration of all things according to their earnest desire.

John Calvin, *Commentary on the Book of Psalms*, trans. Rev. James Anderson (Grand Rapids, MI: Baker Book House, reprint, 1979), Vol. IV, p. 58.

Martin Luther wrote that in the resurrection people will "play with heaven and earth, the sun and all the creatures." And "All creatures shall have their fun, love and joy and shall laugh with thee and thou with them . . . ." Quoted in Jürgen Moltmann, *Theology and Joy*, trans. Reinhard Ulrich (London: SCM Press, LTD, 1973), p. 57.

[56] Emil Brunner, *The Divine Imperative*, trans. Olive Wyon, (The Westminster Press: Philadelphia, 1947), p. 128.

www.ingramcontent.com/pod-product-compliance
Lightning Source LLC
Chambersburg PA
CBHW061741020426
42331CB00006B/1317